Value-Added Marketing

McGRAW-HILL MARKETING FOR PROFESSIONALS

Series Editor: Patrick Forsyth

Value-Added Marketing

Marketing management for superior results

Torsten H Nilson

McGraw-Hill Book Company

London • New York • St Louis • San Francisco • Auckland • Bogotá
Caracas • Hamburg • Lisbon • Madrid • Mexico • Milan • Montreal
New Delhi • Panama • Paris • San Juan • São Paulo • Singapore
Sydney • Tokyo • Toronto

Published by
McGRAW-HILL Book Company Europe
Shoppenhangers Road, Maidenhead, Berkshire, SL6 2QL, England
Telephone 0628 23432
Fax 0628 770224

British Library Cataloguing in Publication Data
Nilson, Torsten H.
 Value-Added Marketing : Marketing
 Management for Superior Results. –
 (McGraw-Hill Marketing for Professionals
 Series)
 I. Title II. Series
 658.8
 ISBN 0-07-707655-9
Library of Congress Cataloging-in-Publication Data
Nilson, Torsten H.
 Value-added marketing : marketing management for superior results
 / Torsten H. Nilson.
   p.   cm. – McGraw-Hill marketing for professionals)
 Includes index.
 ISBN 0-07-707655-9
 1. Marketing – Management. I. Title. II. Series.
HF5415.13.N54 1992
658.8 – dc20   92–9510

1234 CUP 9432

Typeset by Cambridge Composing (UK) Limited
and printed and bound in Great Britain at the University Press,
Cambridge

To Annika, Towe, Bobo, Finn and Tord

Contents

Foreword

This is no ordinary book about marketing. Torsten Nilson provides an insider's experience gained over many years in marketing management positions in fast-moving consumer goods companies in several European markets. It is rare to find someone from this profession who is prepared to take the time to conceptualize his extensive experience in an easy-to-read style.

The book is rich in detail and has a conceptual approach, which is unusual as most marketing texts are written by academics without practical experience, or practising managers without conceptual ability.

Torsten Nilson challenges the commonly held assumptions of marketing as practised by FMCG companies. This unique book is not just about what not to do, but is detailed about what direction the marketing profession should take. It challenges the typical reliance of marketing in FMCG on image-creating variables and advocates making stronger use of the product development function to add value to existing products.

This book should be compulsory reading for marketing professionals at all levels, particularly those engaged in FMCG. Experienced professionals will find that the book challenges their long-held assumptions about how marketing should be undertaken. Newcomers will find the complete coverage of major issues beneficial as it offers excellent insights into a world that is not normally open to outsiders. It should also be read by senior management who need to interact with the marketing function, and product development and production executives who interact regularly with marketing. Finally, professionals in a wide range of marketing services, who have FMCG companies among their clients, would be well advised to read this unique book.

Jean-Pierre Jeannet

Professor of Marketing and Global Business Strategies
IMD, International Management Development Institute
Lausanne, Switzerland

Walter H. Carpenter Professor of Marketing and International Business
Babson College, Wellesley, Massachusetts

Preface

The primary objective of this book is to be an inspiration and catalyst for change. Marketing is an exciting business with many very skilled practitioners, but during the 1980s it would appear that the profession has lost its way. Marketing needs to develop and to progress from the outdated theories of the 1960s. This is my contribution: value-added marketing, a contemporary marketing concept.

The concept is the result of observing successful and not so successful companies in combination with my own experiences as an international FMCG marketing professional. The core message is that the marketing people must focus their attention not on 'fulfilling customers' needs', but on ensuring that the products offer the potential customers superior perceived value for money. I have also concluded that the most sensible and profitable way of achieving that objective is to improve existing products and concepts rather than launch new ones. It is a dynamic, proactive, positive and practical approach, based not so much on an academic analysis as on common sense and commercial experience.

A concept is not useful unless it can be implemented successfully. That is why I have elaborated on how to analyse and apply value-added marketing, providing a framework for the marketers of the future, and mixing the theory with advice and recommendations. I hope that the illustrations, the explanations and the suggestions will add useful information and make the concept more interesting and appealing.

A disclaimer: please note that I have used the word 'product' in a generic sense. Most, if not all, value-added marketing applies to the service industry as well as the product industry, so, if appropriate, please exchange the word product for services.

I have written the book with the 'average' marketing executive in mind, but I think the contents, the theory as well as the advice on application, are relevant for all marketing professionals from the board director to the assistant brand manager, as well as the marketing student. If I have been over-zealous in explaining professional expressions, please accept my apologies; if terminology has been left unexplained, I have done so to avoid boring those with marketing knowledge.

I have enjoyed writing the book, and I hope you and your company will benefit from value-added marketing.

Torsten H. Nilson
Oxted, Surrey, 1992

Acknowledgements

I would like to thank everyone who has made this book possible. I am grateful to all my colleagues who, over the years – knowingly or unknowingly – have contributed with views and ideas that I have used in formulating and explaining my approach to marketing.

I also wish to acknowledge the various sources I have used for my examples, in particular *The Economist, Financial Times, Fortune, The Wall Street Journal, Lebensmittelzeitung, Harvard Business Review* and the UK trade journals *Marketing, Marketing Week, Supermarketing* and *The Grocer*.

The facts behind the Nescafé story are mostly from the MMC report of 1990 and additional information from Mr Frank Edwards, previously chairman and managing director of The Nestlé Company Ltd, and Mr Eddie Humphries, general marketing manager of The Nestlé Company Ltd, has been very useful. The Volvo Corporation in Göteborg, Sweden, has been very helpful in providing additional information on after-sales service and repeat purchase rates. The Benihana example in Chapter 4 is, to a large extent, based on facts I picked up when attending IMEDE (now IMD) in Lausanne, Switzerland. The McDonald's example in Chapter 10 is mainly based on the book *Behind the Arches* by John F. Love. I have also, like so many before me, been stimulated by books by Tom Peters and Robert Waterman, in particular their *In Search of Excellence*.

Among all the people who have inspired me to write this book I would particularly like to thank Mr Barry Brooks for his comments and encouragement. His advice, especially after my first draft, has been invaluable.

Of course much of the credit must go to my wife Annika and my children for tolerating the many hours I spent in front of a word processor instead of working on our house. A special credit is also due to my daughter, Towe, who helped me with the idiosyncracies of the English language.

Finally, I am grateful to Ms Kate Allen and her colleagues at McGraw-Hill for their encouragement and advice.

1

Is marketing an efficient profession?

One of the most dramatic changes to the corporate landscape over the last 40 years has been the introduction of marketing or, more correctly, the introduction of marketing departments. Marketing as such – that is, the skill to make your products attractive for the prospective customers – is an ancient art but as a profession in its own right it is young.

Marketing soon took on the image of being the catalyst for making companies more competitive and profitable. While it undoubtedly is true that the marketing-led companies were very successful initially, it is equally true that over the last decade they have not fared as well on the competitive battlefield.

One can make comparisons on different levels and in different ways. The total level of competitiveness of a country is aggregated in the balance of trade figures. It is fair to state that the US and the UK are the two countries with the greatest number of highly advanced marketing-led companies. Marketing originated in the US and the UK was the first country in Europe to take the concept seriously. This, for instance, is reflected in the generally accepted superiority of the advertising agencies in London and New York.

This superiority in the application of marketing ought to be reflected on the micro as well as the macro level of economics, but balance of trade figures show that both the US and the UK have lost worldwide market share in manufactured goods, as measured by GATT. From 1980 to 1988 the US share declined by 14 per cent, going from 13.1 to 11.3 per cent, and the UK share declined by 24 per cent, from 7.4 to 5.6 per cent of the world market. During the same period Japan's share increased by 13 per cent while West Germany's was virtually static. Taking a longer perspective, in the early 1950s the US and the UK each held about 25 per cent of total world trade in manufactured goods; now, in combination, they only hold around 17 per cent.

The countries gaining share are clearly not those with a tradition of clever marketing, but a tradition of producing consumer goods in an efficient and reliable way. If marketing in its traditional form had been the key factor for success in the 1980s, as we were led to believe, the figures for the US and the UK should have been much more positive.

The balance of trade figures, of course, reflect a country's ability to use marketing techniques, but the figures are also influenced by a number of factors outside any marketers' control. There is, however, ample anecdotal industry-wide evidence to support the point made above, i.e. that marketing-led businesses have not been able to compete successfully with new entrants into their markets.

The most striking example is the car industry. During the 1960s and 1970s, Ford and GM were heralded as companies who really had taken marketing to their hearts and were using all modern theories and techniques to launch and market the 'right' products. The result is well known to everyone. The US car industry has consistently lost market share over the last decades, not only internationally but more significantly in its own country. One car in three bought in the US is Japanese, and in trend-setting California the total Japanese market share is around 40 per cent, the only brand not being out-sold by the foreign invasion being Chevrolet. There must obviously be something that marketers can learn from the management approach of these relative newcomers.

Even the very large multi-national FMCG (fast-moving consumer goods) companies have not been particularly successful. They do not manage to expand their businesses (excluding acquisitions) in the developed world by more than a few percentage points per annum, despite having huge resources at hand. In some markets, such as frozen foods, they have even lost share to smaller and less 'sophisticated' competitors. Just as the US car industry, these companies have been regarded over the years as super marketers, but the big gains in the marketplace have often been elusive.

The retail trade in the UK represents a striking contrast to the FMCG giants. One of the most high-ranking brands in the UK is the retailer Marks & Spencer with its own label St Michael. Various surveys have shown that the consumers rank M&S/St Michael as one of the most trusted and accepted brands. M&S do not advertise in the UK to any significant degree, and set up their first marketing department in 1985, so the success is certainly not 'marketing department-led'.

Another major UK retailer, J Sainsbury's, provides us with a similar example. While the M&S product range is 100 per cent under private label, Sainsbury's is less so, 60–70 per cent, but in many market segments their private label has both higher acceptance and better sales than most proprietary brands. Marks & Spencer and J Sainsbury's have both had growth rates far superior to the majority of the larger FMCG companies, who have in many instances lost the initiative and with it market positions and consumer confidence. The retailers have been more successful in building a strong position with the consumers.

One factor that can be eliminated in our search for reasons for a lack of success is the quality of the marketing executives. Virtually all blue chip FMCG companies have managements and marketing staff that are of the highest calibre. The marketers are, with few exceptions, bright, talented, energetic and hungry for success. They have tremendous financial resources at their disposal and have access to the best advertising agencies in the world. The practitioners are not lacking in ability, but *what* they are doing and the *way* they are marketing the products form the reason for their relatively poor results.

Development over the last 10 years has not been encouraging. Given the amount and quality of human, technical and financial resources, classical marketing-led companies should be much more successful than they are. The change from a growth environment, where marketing in its classical form was a useful management technique, to a stagnating and more competitive business scene has meant that classical marketing-led businesses no longer have the upper hand. These companies have lost out to entrepreneurial and product/quality-led competitors. Given the resources and the talent, the large companies should by now have eliminated these competitors, but that certainly has not happened.

I am convinced that marketing, if correctly applied, can play an enormously important role in a company. It is equally obvious that the solution to the apparent lack of marketing efficiency is not to abandon the concept of marketing but to improve it. The marketing profession must change and become more aggressive and more skilled; above all it must concentrate on the issues that will lead to success.

I began this project on the definition and application of value-added marketing because I had reached the conclusion over several years of marketing management that the profession needed a relaunch. The basic marketing theory of fulfilling needs and wants has passed its 'sell by' date. To gain market share in an increasingly competitive world, a revision of the marketing concept is necessary.

Marketing should be the life-blood of an organization. I hope that the contents of this book will provide a transfusion of new ideas to the marketing profession, and that the concept and the methods I have developed will make marketing in *your* company more efficient. If you wish to avoid being overtaken, you must continuously improve.

2

The weaknesses of classical marketing

In the first chapter I described briefly how marketing failed to be the 'key factor for success' during the 1980s. Although it is non-productive to dwell on this lost opportunity, it is essential to review the background if we are to build a new framework.

The marketing concept, which developed out of the post-war boom in the US, had undoubtedly a tremendous impact on the business community when it was first introduced and applied. It was adapted and developed by the then leading consumer goods companies and became, for many, the symbol of a modern, progressive enterprise. These first-wave marketing-led companies were successful, for although marketing in this form certainly had its shortcomings, it was a vast improvement on the functional approach that had, until then, been the norm.

The base for any analysis of marketing as we know it, 'classical marketing', has to be Philip Kotler's marketing textbook *Marketing Management*, which is the 'bible' for anyone working or planning a career in marketing. The definition of marketing in Kotler's books is certainly the one that is most used. Although the concept has been modified over the years from a simple statement about satisfying 'the needs and wants' to achieving the 'desired satisfactions more effectively and efficiently', the basic idea remains unchanged, that is, that success depends on the ability to define and fulfil the customers' needs and wants. The marketing concept in more everyday language, and how it is practised today, is that by satisfying the consumers' – or, more precisely, the customers' – needs and wants the company will be profitable and, by implication, the more the customers are satisfied, the higher the profits.

At the core of the concept is the assumption that there are a sufficient number of unfulfilled needs to ensure a long-term

business development, and that filling those needs is the best way
to deploy the company's (marketing) resources.

New product development

There are many aspects of fulfilling 'needs and wants'. One cynical
comment is that if you have commercially significant needs and
wants waiting to be fulfilled, you are unlikely to have the money to
pay for the goods and services to fill those needs!

A more serious and generally applicable point is that almost all of
the more basic needs, and most of the not-so-basic ones, have
already been met by past generations of skilled marketers. This is in
sharp contrast to the situation when the marketing concept was first
introduced. At that time there were many empty gaps in the market,
but most of these, though not all, have now been filled.

The 'supporting evidence' for this statement can be found in the
dismal success record of new product development (NPD) activities
in the FMCG market. Thousands of products are introduced each
year. In the USA in 1988, some 8000 new food products were
introduced. In Europe the numbers are smaller but new products
are still seen as a very important part of the marketing mix.

From a classical marketing point of view this strategy makes sense.
A new product is the obvious answer to an unfulfilled need as it
immediately satisfies and fills the gap.

One must also realize that one of the main tasks of marketing
executives is to find these needs and wants, and they will do
everything in their power to define and create a market opportunity,
and thus prove their skills. The needs thus defined can only be
fulfilled by either the launch of a new product or the repositioning
of an existing one. As most executives, and their superiors, like to
minimize risks and believe in market growth, they usually choose
the new product alternative. It is widely believed that a new product
is more likely to expand the market, while a change to an existing
product carries the risk that not only can the new positioning fail,
but existing sales could also be damaged.

This method of operation makes the whole marketing department
very NPD biased. In addition, based on the knowledge that the
introduction of new products have caused market growth and sales
success in the past, new products have been seen as the saviour, the
magic, that will solve a company's problems. The vast number of

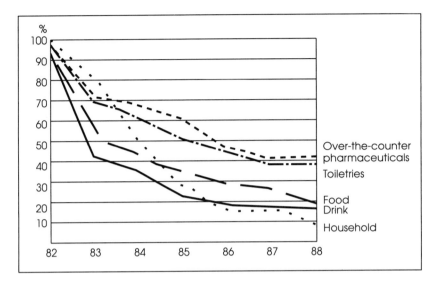

Figure 2.1 Percentage of all 1982 new product launches surviving until 1988 (*Source*: Goodall Alexander O'Hare)

products that have failed, and the cost behind the development work and the launches, is often forgotten.

Research reports are published from time to time which show the poor success rate of new product launches. The reports generally show that only around 10 per cent of the projects initiated ever materialize. Not a very impressive record! When it comes to the real test in the marketplace, a study in the UK in 1989 showed that of 3458 products launched in the FMCG market, only 29 per cent survived the first two years. The main reason for this low success rate is that the market now has very few gaps that are big enough to justify a new product.

So entrenched are the FMCG companies in the philosophy that 'new product development' is the way to expand a business that, despite diminishing return on investments in the launch of new products, the number of products launched has grown virtually year by year over the last two decades. More and more resources are channelled into a type of activity that is unlikely to generate large revenues.

Gaps in the market

An example that shows the dangers of adapting classical marketing principles, and basing a strategy on assumed unfulfilled consumer needs, is the attack many financial institutions made on the estate agent market in the UK. During the latter part of the 1980s the estate agent market was swallowed by these institutions. Banks, building societies and insurance companies spent almost £2 billion buying into the market. They saw a 'need' and a gap in the market to offer financial services along with a house purchase. A very 'clever' idea, as the purchase of a house is almost always connected with some form of financial service – insurance and mortgage being the two most important. What the institutions failed to understand, or thought they could overcome, was that the estate agents were not very credible partners. The connection institution/estate agent tended to devalue rather than add value to the financial services that could be offered. The one value customers like to see in someone who is dealing with their finances is trust and objectivity, which, unfortunately, are not the stronger points in the estate agent's public image. A straightforward piece of customer market research showed that in 1989 only about 10 per cent of potential house buyers were willing to use an estate agent for mortgage advice; and for building and contents insurance the figure was even lower. Considerably more than 10 per cent of the sample said that they wanted to avoid using an estate agent for anything other than buying a property.

The result of the strategy was that many institutions lost considerable amounts of money – hundreds of millions of pounds – on their ventures into the estate agent market.

A clearer understanding of the house-buying customer and the marketplace would have made it possible to avoid a very expensive lesson. The unfulfilled market niche/need that the financial services companies defined was of no interest to the customers. The companies paid an excessive price for estate agents because they thought the new channels would open up a new segment of the market. But the estate agents were not credible channels through which to sell financial products, so the connection with estate agents added no value to the product – rather the reverse, as shown by the lack of success.

The main weaknesses

The main reasons for the disappointing results of classical marketing are that marketing:

- is reactive, not proactive

- is slow, not fast

- encourages creativity at the expense of business sense and experience

- is based on market growth rather than defending market share in a stagnating market.

Classical marketing is by definition *reactive*. The objective of the marketer, according to the theory, is to search for and define unfulfilled needs. The marketer can and will only deal with the current situation, because in order to fulfil a need (or a want) it has to exist. If it does not exist it cannot be defined, so each decision has to be based on observations of the 'current' world.

This makes marketing a reflection of what has happened. The marketer becomes conditioned to react to the environment rather than be proactive and develop the market and the products beyond the demands of the present situation (and the customers' views on the day they were subjected to market research).

The initiative and leadership are relegated to a creative and intellectual analysis of the marketplace rather than taking the philosophy of the entrepreneur who will have a vision of how the products should be developed and will move in that direction.

A second problem with classical marketing is that it is *slow*. The traditional management way to resolve such a problem would be to implement systems to speed up the process with activities such as strong follow-up programmes, accountability to general management regarding the timing, cutting of management layers, etc. Unfortunately the introduction of such activities, although necessary in many instances, will be like easing the symptom rather than curing the disease. It will not cure the real problem, as it does not attack the cause. The 'cause' is that modern, well-educated marketing people have built-in delay factors because of their training. That is not only a conclusion based on logic; experience supports the statement.

The logical side of the argument is as follows: to identify a need, the marketer has to search for it. When the search phase is over, and the executive has found a market gap, he or she has to define the market opportunity and research it. On the basis of those results, the marketer will develop a product or a service to fulfil the need, will again research the product to ensure that it really meets the need, will conclude all thoughts and analyses in a marketing plan and, finally, will launch the product. Obviously this whole process takes time. Also, by its very nature and length, it fosters an environment that is far removed from the dynamic thrust that should be the trade mark of a modern business.

Another way to look at this aspect of classical marketing is to observe the large marketing-led companies. A superficial analysis shows that they are certainly not first off the mark and rarely take the initiative to 'rock the boat' by moving the market forward with real, exciting product improvements. Admittedly this has sometimes been to their advantage, as the slowness in itself has meant that they have avoided jumping on opportunities that proved to be shortlived.

The following example illustrates the sweeping statement above. The biggest frozen food company in Europe is Unilever, trading under a number of brands such as Iglo in Germany, France and Holland, and Birds Eye in the UK. The Unilever group allocates a lot of resources to product development and research (approximately £395 million) and, according to public statements, place great emphasis on developing the market. 'The quality, safety and appeal of our products . . . can only be guaranteed and enhanced by substantial investment in research and development' (Unilever Annual Report, 1989). As a regular observer of the Dutch–British consumer goods giant, I do not think there is any reason to doubt the commitment expressed in the 1989 annual report. Despite the above-mentioned resources and the very qualified managements of the Unilever group, it has been surprisingly unsuccessful in launching in the frozen foods market new products representing real successful innovations. The market position has been maintained only in the market segments where Unilever has a solid foundation (such as fish fingers, vegetables and traditional ready meals). On the other hand, Unilever Germany has failed to be competitive in the fastest growing segment of the market: pizzas.

Ten years ago Iglo was the brand leader, but due to lack of interest or ability Iglo invested neither sufficient time nor effort to produce a better product. The competitors took a different view. The main one, Dr Oetker, started to make better value products. The Oetker company did not invent really new products – after all, a pizza is a pizza – but it improved and improved the pizza and added interesting taste variants. Today it is the indisputed brand leader.

Almost all of the growth sectors of the frozen food market have been exploited by smaller companies. These smaller operations have been more flexible and have had a greater ability to predict, or perhaps to understand, future developments. The progressive ideas have come from mid-sized companies such as Findus and Ross (now UB) in the UK and the above-mentioned Dr Oetker in Germany. More development has also come from smaller companies (Dalepak, Tiffany's, Freshbake) and from such retailers as Marks & Spencer and J Sainsbury's in the UK and Bofrost and Eismann in Germany. (The latter organizations are certainly large, but cannot be characterized as classically marketing-led companies.) The consequences have been that Unilever has seen its brand share deteriorate quite dramatically in its two major markets, the UK and western Germany. Over the last 10 years Birds Eye's market share in the UK has gone from 32 to 20 per cent and Iglo in Germany has had a similar development, with the market share declining from 28 per cent in 1984 to 17 per cent only six years later.

Classical marketing is based on the principle of finding unexploited market segments. The search for unfulfilled needs and wants is the basis for the work of the marketing executive. The successful follower of this principle has to be *creative*. The analytical process that leads to the definition of a new market segment or position requires a creative mind. As a consequence, the marketing departments are filled with people constantly looking at products and markets in a 'new' way rather than spending time on learning the business properly and building up operational experience. It has to be stated, of course, that there is no disadvantage in being creative. The problem is that if creativity is emphasized, as it is today, and is considered to be a key skill, then other skills such as numeracy and product knowledge are less well represented.

The most serious consequence of the emphasis on creativity is that another dimension suffers: experience. To be able to run a business successfully you have to know it. To get to know it takes time, and marketing executives are rarely given that time.

EXAMPLE It is a fact that you must know your profession if you are to be successful. There is no reason for the marketing profession to be different from any other. For instance, who would you prefer to take out your inflamed appendix: a surgeon with 10 years' experience or someone straight out of medical school? Or would you not prefer a doctor who has done 100 such operations rather than one who has just started doing appendectomies but was previously a specialist fixing broken collar bones? To make the example complete, I am sure you would not be interested in having the operation done by a retired surgeon of many years experience, who has not operated for some time and has failing eyesight and shaking hands!

The quest for creativity at the expense of business experience is striking when one reads the appointments pages in marketing journals. It seems that most companies consider marketing to be an exception to all other professions, as less experienced people are preferred over those with many years of duty behind them. It is not possible to get a degree, accumulate a lot of experience and still fit into a requested age profile of 25–30 years old! Similarly, when the young marketing executives are planning their careers, job changes appear to be more important than solid knowledge achieved by staying in the same job for several years. In the short term it is perhaps not as glamorous to stay put, and salary increases might be lower, but for the corporation, and in the long term for the individual, it is more advantageous as I shall explain later.

To achieve real success, it is necessary to have real knowledge, and that takes time. Almost all companies that are successful over the longer term have senior managers who have been with the company for many years and know what they are doing. There are, of course, many well-publicized cases where an outside chief executive has taken over and achieved excellent results. But in virtually all of those cases the rest of the senior management has remained unchanged. The new CEO becomes the catalyst, bringing out the talent and knowledge of that existing management.

Marketers, as most other professions, like to use sophisticated examples. On the other hand, in many situations the simple, straightforward solutions and examples are the best. In my view the marketing executive can learn a lot from people who, with instant feedback, deal directly with their customers.

EXAMPLE   Successful street traders can give many clues on how marketing people should regard their work. Good street traders know all about their merchandise, its strong points and its weak points. If they are vegetable traders they know where the potatoes come from, and the type of tomatoes on display. The traders know how the tomatoes taste and how ripe they are. They know their (local) markets, the prices the competitors charge and what other traders are good at, and not so good at. They also know their customers, perhaps by name, and certainly by sight. If they have an opportunity to discover names, they remember them and use them as often as possible, to personalize their communication. They are honest, because if they cheat their customers, those customers will not come back; but, of course, they always present their goods in the best possible way. They only use arguments that they know, from experience, give a sale.

All these are simple rules, based on experience and knowledge, and they apply to the modern mass communication marketing world as well as to the Surrey Street vegetable market in the London Borough of Croydon.

The examples of the surgeon and the street traders are mentioned because they make the point that experience is an essential part of any success story. Comprehensive knowledge and thorough experience are key factors for success in all professions. Marketing is no exception.

Another almost forgotten factor is 'business sense'. It is difficult to define business sense; it is a combination of talent and acquired knowledge and skills. Although only a few are born entrepreneurs, the trained marketer can learn from such people. The marketer will be able to run a much more efficient commercial operation by combining an acquired business sense with experience and theoretical training than by spending time and energy on being creative in defining market niches.

There exists an under-current of growing dissatisfaction with marketing executives for many different reasons, some of which I have listed above. A study by McKinsey in the US showed substantial dissatisfaction with marketers. CEOs and senior marketing executives of 18 leading packaged goods companies were interviewed, and dissatisfaction was expressed on a number of dimensions including new and established product development, decision making and risk management. One major reason is that the marketing theory of the past has taken precedence over sound commercial management in the training of young marketers. Consequently, senior management are disappointed and the business is suffering.

At the time of the 'launch' of the classical marketing concept most markets were in a *growth* phase. In the post-1945 society there were many opportunities to exploit in the marketplace and it was possible to find new and creative ways of selling products. In such a dynamic environment the classical marketing techniques were quite appropriate, especially given the previous production-led and functional approach.

Since the 1970s the western consumer goods markets have experienced a slowing down in growth rates, and in today's world they have reached very low figures or are even *stagnating* totally. The cake that is available for sharing is not getting bigger, but companies wishing to be part of the sharing are growing in number and are becoming more and more aggressive. To be successful the marketing strategy has to change from one of encouraging and exploiting market growth to one of fighting for market share and defending the market position.

Society has gone through a tremendous change since the start of the US concept of marketing. At the time the consumer markets were blossoming and there were plenty of unfulfilled needs. The consumers were keen to consume more of everything. During the 1980s, and certainly also during the 1990s, this is changing. Today's caring generation is not looking for more of everything, it is looking for getting more out of what is already there, i.e. a better quality of life.

The relative usefulness of classical marketing has declined, because we have moved from a situation of market growth to one of fighting for market share. In a growth environment the strategy to look for unfulfilled needs and wants makes a lot of sense. Why fight for old ground when you can go for virgin territory? The problem is that there is less and less virgin territory around in western Europe and North America. Thus, defending and increasing your market share becomes much more important.

Segmentation and economies of scale

'Market segmentation' has been a buzz phrase in marketing ever since classical marketing was introduced and the emphasis on segmentation is behind many of the inefficiencies of classical marketing. We have in many markets an over-segmentation, which is devaluing the products as the cost for the segmentation outweighs the benefits for the customers. It is an over-segmentation in both product formulation and communication.

According to economic theory the cost of segmentation has to be less than the revenue it generates. In other words, the extra costs that the segmentation will cause through shorter production runs, more expensive advertising, extended stock holding, etc., has to be balanced by an increase in revenue, either through higher sales or better margins. That is seldom the case as the additional margins and sales are usually fairly limited and the costs of product proliferation can be significant. Segmentation can even lead to loss of sales. If, after the segmentation process, the product range is not perceived to be a really better value-for-money offer, it is not credible with the consumers. An even more likely development is that the business base for each segment becomes so small that the products are discontinued by the distributors and/or are not big enough to generate the necessary volumes for efficient communication and production. The result is an over-segmented product group.

Most, but not all, FMCG marketers have over the years almost totally ignored the effects of economies of scale in communication and production. The volume effect makes it possible to generate higher margins that can be reinvested in communication or product improvements or, alternatively, to keep the selling prices attractive and, in that way, keep out aggressive competitors. The value-for-money dimension has been ignored at the expense of having product ranges with variants fitting every conceivable need.

An exception

It has to be said that even if society is changing and classical marketing is becoming obsolete, there is still room for classical marketing successes. One such example is the Unilever shampoo Timotei, designed and launched around the need for a mild shampoo to fit the then emerging habit of washing hair every day.

EXAMPLE   Timotei is a brilliant example of the classical marketing theory: define a need (a shampoo for everyday use), develop a product, launch it with consistent marketing support (packaging as well as advertising) and then, when it is well established, extend the concept to related products (such as conditioners) so that the economies of scale in the advertising are maximized. The idea was born in one country, and when its success became apparent, and when conditions in other countries allowed it, the concept was internationalized.

If there were many more examples like Timotei, Unilever would be an even bigger company and there would be no reason to define a new marketing concept.

Conclusion

The work of Philip Kotler and other marketing prophets has obviously been of great importance. The companies that initially followed the marketing principles were successful because these principles were certainly better than the previous functional approach.

For the 1990s we have to go beyond the concept of classical marketing as it is no longer sufficient for a successful strategy. A new marketing concept has to be defined; one that will offer the companies a more businesslike approach. An approach that will

- make the companies proactive, not reactive
- be fast, not slow
- encourage business values, not creativity
- be suitable for a market share strategy
- avoid unnecessary niche marketing
- make sure that customers get a better deal.

3

Marketing and the world: the interaction

Business is an integral and important part of society. Everyone is directly or indirectly connected to the business world – directly as proprietors or employees, indirectly as customers or participants in the service functions of local and central government. Therefore, it is not surprising that the general trends in the community will reflect on the business world.

The relationship between society and business is particularly relevant to marketing, as that is supposed to be the part of the company closest to the man or woman on the street, the consumer. If marketing, as a discipline, is to be contemporary and not fall behind, it has to be consistent with what is happening in the real world.

There are two aspects of this statement. Firstly, if marketing is to be efficient in a commercial sense it has to be in phase with the total social environment, otherwise marketing will not be able to play its part in progressing the working methods of the companies concerned. Secondly, if marketing is to be responsible for moving the company's products in the most appropriate direction, it has to be in tune with what the potential customers think and do, otherwise the marketers will make the wrong decisions.

Many social trends (and even more short-term fads) have emerged over the years that have elapsed since marketing was first introduced in Europe. These changes have not affected marketing theory or application to any significant degree, which is surprising when one takes into account that the people who are active in marketing are, with few exceptions, very much up to date on current trends in a general sense. One has to note, though, that considerable progress has taken place in the areas of marketing 'workmanship' – that is, research techniques and analytical tools have been refined; the advertising development process has been made different, and better; the new product development programmes have more distinct targets, etc. – but the basic marketing theory is still the same.

The historical context

The need for a business to stay in tune with the society around it, and the interaction between society and the business world, is nothing new.

The most fundamental change to business practices, after the introduction of money, came in the late eighteenth and early nineteenth century with the introduction of 'free' trade, inspired and influenced by Adam Smith's *An Inquiry into the Nature and Causes of the Wealth of Nations*, published in 1776. Adam Smith's main message was that the dynamics of the commercial environment is such that if it is left alone it will 'automatically' generate the best value at the lowest possible price, thus creating maximum wealth for the nation. Government should let the invisible hand (= market forces) do the controlling, instead of government officials and guilds. Such thoughts, revolutionary at the time, were consistent with, and a reflection of, the general philosophical sentiments of the second half of the eighteenth century.

The interaction between society and the commercial world plays an important role in the development of business concepts. The development of classical marketing was a reflection of the sentiments 40 years ago, and while the marketing concept was consistent with the general environment through the 1950s and 1960s, it later became dissonant and during the 1980s the consequences of a stagnating marketing concept became apparent as the marketing-led companies started to lose their competitive advantages. For the 1990s a new approach to marketing will be needed as society continues to change.

The first phase of marketing

Originally, before classical marketing was introduced, the task for the marketing function (or its equivalent) was to find ways of selling the goods the company's factories produced. The consumer society was in its infancy and to be successful it was sufficient to have an efficient manufacturing and distribution organization. There was considerable growth in the various market sectors of the consumer goods companies, which was a significant advantage as it is always easier to share a growing cake. In addition, there was less pressure on the FMCG companies from suppliers and customers (the retail trade), as they were also enjoying a growth environment. The purpose of the marketing departments, if they existed at all, was simply to ensure that the products of the company were sold. In principle, and with the benefit of hindsight, a fairly easy task. What it did demand, and what the marketing personnel had to excel in, was creativity in the promotional field. As it was outside of the responsibility of the marketing people to be involved in the product itself, creativity focused around *how* to sell. This era generated virtually all the promotional techniques that we still use – couponing, money-back guarantees, sampling – and it also put the focus on the ability to create striking advertising. While it is easy to be arrogant about the past, one has to recognize that, because of the single-mindedness of the marketing activities, excellent advertising was produced and a lot of creativity was generated in devising various promotional ideas. Because of the functional, non-integrated approach the whole organization was compartmentalized and the marketing activities focused on only one thing, short-term sales. On the other hand, it was quite efficient in that the functions had clear, single-minded objectives and the functional approach fostered professionalism within the disciplines. The lesson to learn from this first phase is that professionalism is the foundation for sound business development and the need for it is timeless. This was the first phase of marketing management.

The second phase of marketing

The basic approach to marketing was not enough when the post-war society started to blossom, first in North America and later in Europe.

During the 1950s the western world experienced the first truly affluent society. The average man had a chance to live in a way that was considered total luxury just 50 years, or less, earlier. This development came first to the US, as it had emerged relatively undamaged from the Second World War. Western and northern Europe needed another 5–10 years to catch up after the destruction from the war. Mass marketing flourished to fulfil the growing demand. The classical marketing techniques of segmentation and fitting the product to the consumers' demands made the progressive FMCG companies very successful.

During the mid-1960s a new trend developed with more concern for the world, for 'peace' and for general spiritual well-being. The superficial materialism of the 1950s was felt to be insufficient. This culminated in the 'revolutions' of 1968. Marketing adapted and became more sophisticated, but was also more criticized. As a marketer one had to be more thoughtful; it was not enough to be creative in a hard-hitting way. Everyone was looking for clever, less brash, ideas such as the classical VW launch campaign in the US described later in the book.

This second phase of marketing development saw the introduction of the now classical marketing concept. At the time it was revolutionary. It moved the emphasis from the company to the customer. It was a truly non-functional concept in that it emphasized integrated marketing in which all functions in the company were to be market-oriented and it emphasized the necessity to change and adapt to the customers' needs and wants. Professor Philip Kotler was, and is, the 'Prophet' of modern marketing due to his textbooks on the subject and virtually all large consumer goods companies around the globe, such as Unilever, Nestlé, Procter & Gamble and Colgate-Palmolive, became his disciples.

One significant internal effect in these companies was the power that was transferred from the functional organization to the marketing departments. The brand manager became the key person. Everything centred around the brand manager, who, at least in theory, was responsible for managing the brand or product. The brand manager's role was, and still is, defined as to interpret what the consumer would like to have. The brand manager had, and often still has, the responsibility of guiding the company's total resources towards the goal of fulfilling the consumers' needs – obviously, or perhaps hopefully, under the supervision of senior management.

The objective with this management philosophy is that through the adaptation of marketing the whole organization becomes sensitive to what the consumer would like to have and strives towards fulfilling those needs. By fulfilling those needs it is assumed that the company becomes more profitable. The entire concept made sense at the time, seen against the previous much less integrated and customer-oriented approach. The initial success of the companies that adapted the method became a further endorsement of the theory.

The success of the classical marketing concept was one more facet of the in-flow of ideas from the US into Europe and other parts of the world. In the post-war world the US was the inspiration for business people from all over the globe. The US multi-nationals dominated the scene and were considered a threat to the rest of the world. Jean-Jacques Servan-Schreiber's *Le défit américain* became a best seller. The debate raged on whether the US multi-nationals would one day take over the world. The debate did not consider that to win you have to adapt, and not many years elapsed before the competitive scene changed dramatically. The US multi-nationals started to come under severe pressure from, in particular, the Japanese companies.

One cannot disregard the impact of the American way of doing business, as it gave the European corporate scene a very healthy kick in the 1950s and 1960s. Many lessons were learned, one of the most important certainly being the application of marketing.

Marketing in the 1970s and 1980s

After the 'glorious' days of classical marketing came the 1970s. Although it was a fairly pessimistic decade, it left its mark on business. Or was it perhaps the business problems that made the decade so miserable? Also during the 1970s there was an obvious interaction between society and marketing. Marketing suffered from the 'hang-over' of 1968 and the oil crises of that period made the profession's main tool, advertising, a fairly rare commodity as many companies decreased their spend to boost short-term profits. This decade gave the first indications that all was not well in the marketing world. For instance, the dramatic changes of 1973 discarded much of the long-term planning and confidence received its first dent.

Finally, in the yuppie eighties, the entrepreneur was king. Make money for yourself, be rich, enjoy it and be proud of it! Certainly not a way of life that would have been acceptable to the 'Flower Power' generation in 1968, but 20 years later it was well accepted. The changing society left the marketers with great expectations but the results were less impressive. Short-termism invaded marketing and, at least in the UK, marketing staff became extremely mobile, which meant that staff with a genuine knowledge of specific market sectors became a scarce commodity.

During the 1970s, and especially the 1980s, the positive competitive effects of classical marketing generally disappeared. Firstly, as most companies had adapted consumer awareness in their business approach, there was no longer a competitive advantage in being sensitive to customers' needs. Secondly, the social and political environment had changed significantly compared to the 1950s and 1960s when marketing first came into its own, so classical marketing was less relevant. The interaction between society, business and marketing came to a halt during these decades and, as a result, marketing became a less efficient contributor to the companies' well-being.

From a world competitive point of view the total American dominance came to an end, and in the 1970s and 1980s the Japanese business world became the focus of attention. The Japanese method of running businesses, and, in particular, the way they were running the big export-driven companies, became almost a cult subject. It became obvious that the American model was no longer the ultimate. Initially, to their great surprise, US and European companies were solidly beaten in a number of product categories: electronics, cars, ship building, etc. It became clear to many that in order to look for inspiration for your business it was not enough to follow the development in America, one had to look at the world outside of the North American continent. Japan, with its extraordinary successes, filled the gap.

The impact of the Japanese way of business life was not as fundamental as the previous concept from the USA because the European commercial world was more developed in the 1970s and 1980s than it had been in the 1950s and 1960s. Years of following the American way of life had matured to a higher level of sophistication, and Europe had totally recovered from the Second World War. The impact of the Japanese system of running companies came more from the example the Japanese set by showing that to succeed you have to do things properly. The real lesson learned – by many the hard way – was that quality and production efficiency are key concepts in achieving an expanding and profitable business.

Background to the third phase of marketing

The social development in the 1990s promises to be more influenced by 'traditional' values. It will become more fashionable to keep to family values, and with the environmental issues there will also be more emphasis on taking care of what we have. Social values follow the trends. For example, AIDS has changed our outlook on promiscuity; it is no longer considered strange to be faithful to your partner. It seems that the trend-setters, although not without exceptions, have finally realized that it is the faithful family husband or wife who has the happiest life. It is he or she who gets the benefit of other people's care and trust. It is also he or she who gets the

Table 3.1 The three phases of marketing

Phase	Activity	Focus
First	Sell	Company
Second	Adapt	Customer
Third	Improve	Competition

opportunity to build something; a family, a home, traditions. Most people have also realized that it takes time to learn how to live in such a society and to achieve a happy life. You have to work at creating happiness, and you must know the people around you before you can do so. That takes time and effort. The caring society is on its way.

Many values change. More of everything is not necessarily the main objective now, because the lives of the consumers are already saturated with goods and services. Today's overflow of goods transforms consumers into 'discriminators' rather than 'needers and wanters'. The consumers do not want another type of shirt, they want a better quality shirt (in its widest sense) at an attractive price. The 'more of everything' attitude is replaced by the more mature outlook of getting more out of each item.

Marketing products in the 1990s will have to follow that trend. The classical marketing solutions of 'fulfilling needs and wants' and 'exploiting new market segments' is totally dissonant with the society of the 1990s in the western world. Marketing needs to take care, develop and nurture to provide the customers with better products and services.

These dynamics in the society demands a development of marketing theory. In addition, the success in recent years of non-classical marketing operations such as Marks & Spencer, Body Shop and other entrepreneurial type organizations, together with the Japanese wave, is a clear sign that a third phase of marketing theory (Table 3.1) is due.

The third phase in marketing has to go beyond just identifying and exploiting the consumers' needs and wants, because that is simply not enough if a company wants to be a strong force in the marketplace. It is not only that the competition is more difficult to deal with; the customers aspire to more than having the FMCG industry fulfilling their 'needs'.

To maintain customer loyalty and gain market share the product and the service has to be better than the available alternatives, and must be improved constantly. How to achieve this is the main factor in the new marketing concept.

The new concept has its foundation in classical marketing, as this has had such a fundamental impact. Classical marketing was once revolutionary, and as it is the base on which current marketing practices are built, it is impossible to ignore. That is why one should understand the past before one is able to develop and fully utilize a new concept.

Conclusion

Classical marketing has had a tremendous impact on the business world ever since its introduction. It developed as a reflection of the situation in the 1950s and 1960s. But during the past decade it has become more and more dissonant and a new phase of marketing is needed for the future.

Europe has always been a continent with a varied and rich cultural and business life. During the 1990s it will probably change beyond recognition, hopefully in a positive sense, and certainly in a way that will influence the rest of the world. The new social and political environment will put increasing pressure on companies to be competitive and to develop in order to take advantage of the opportunities. Any new opportunities will also generate new competitors and, to be successful, companies must ensure that their operations are as efficient and as competitive as possible. The time has come for a marketing concept for the 1990s: a third phase.

4

Competition in a stagnating world market

Business people have always complained that the business climate is becoming more and more competitive. There is no doubt, however, in my mind that the lack of market growth in many sectors over the last decade(s) has made each sale more difficult to close. We have also seen many new entrants into the marketplace, not only from Japan but also from the rising economies of south-east Asia, the so-called Tiger economies. Improved communications and a more competitive stance by many large corporations from all over the world have fuelled the competitive climate. Furthermore, government and EC policies have encouraged competition in a general sense.

In all, a number of different factors have made business life more difficult. The situation is unlikely to change and all businesses have to be more aware of and ready to tackle the competitive threats that exist or will exist in the future.

For the FMCG market the main factor behind the intensified competition is the lack of market growth. In many market sectors of the consumer goods markets there is no growth at all, but almost without exception more companies than previously are competing. Although the total GNP is growing, most of that growth comes from sectors outside of the FMCG markets. The total grocery market, for instance, is growing by no more than a few percentage points each year and subsectors with high growth rates become fewer and smaller.

The statement 'competition has increased and will increase', although true, gives little guidance on *what* to do; it merely states that something must be done. To get an understanding of what to do and how to do it, a study of a few of the successful competitors can be enlightening.

The Japanese wave

During the 1980s we saw the success of many new brands, companies and products. Many of these came from Japan. Several books and articles have been written on how the Japanese approach their chosen markets: the thoroughness, the productivity, the long-term view. There are many lessons to be learned from the Japanese phenomenon, not only in production management, which has been the subject generating the greatest interest, but also for marketers. Many Japanese companies have had extraordinary successes in different types of markets applying straightforward principles of combining customer and product knowledge with outstanding value for money. Although the Japanese have now passed their most impressive growth phase, they still have the ability and ambition to continue to be a real competitive threat to the western business world. According to the Nomura Research Institute, major Japanese companies have switched their investments to an even higher degree into research and development in order to 'make the mousetrap better' and a Japanese government report stated that the investment in R&D in 1990 grew by 14.1 per cent, representing a ratio of 2.91 per cent of the GNP. The majority of the spend was related to innovations in new products and materials. As a comparison, the spend in the US was around 2.5 per cent of the GNP. The market leading companies Hitachi, NEC and Fujitsu all pour around 10 per cent of their sales into research and development. There are a number of reasons for this acceleration in committing resources to research and development: one is that automation requires more R&D, but the main one involves survival tactics for the longer term. 'They are having to add all sorts of hi-tech "smarts" to their products to keep their new and more demanding customers happy', to quote an article in the authoritative magazine *The Economist* in December 1989. The policy is: never be satisfied with the current product and constantly review everything to see if it can be made better. The Japanese even have a term 'miryokuteki hinshitsu' for the activity of examining everything to see if it is being done correctly, and 'correctly' in this context means perfect. For the car companies, Toyota and Honda, such an approach has not only made it possible for them to conquer the mass market, but they are now considered to be a serious threat to the European luxury car industry.

Japanese technology is in many areas considered to be superior to that in America or Europe, but despite this the Japanese continue to invest, and in an accelerating way. The otherwise common tendency to relax and enjoy the sweet smell of success is replaced by an aggressive attitude to ensure that the competitive gap does not shrink.

In order to be successful it is not enough to develop new and better products. They have to be brought to the market, and to achieve that in an efficient way the Japanese have another aspect to their competitive arsenal: 'speed'. One of the major weaknesses of the western marketers is that they are often very slow to introduce improvements and real novelties. It is interesting to note that the technological advantages the large Japanese companies enjoy come not only from the traditional sources such as being innovative and creative but from three factors that are often overlooked, namely, speed, teamwork and confidence. The Japanese companies have realized that there is little point in spending time doing detailed market research studies on the extra features that a new or old product will need to achieve a good sales level. It is much better to rush the ideas into the shops and then, with great attention, monitor what the real customers are saying and doing. This aspect is particularly relevant; the success behind the Japanese wave is partly because the producers have packed the products with extra gadgets or features to enhance the value. Detailed market research takes time, but real in-store checks are quicker and, above all, are more accurate as they represent actual commitments rather than just stated intentions to a market research interviewer. Also, in parallel with testing new features and awaiting the results of the real-life tests, further developments are in progress.

It is not the development in itself that the observers give as the main reason for the success, it is the way the novelties and improvements are brought to the market. Through diligent teamwork the new features are presented to the customers as soon as possible in order to beat the competition. This means that the R&D staff receive feedback much more quickly; they acquire more knowledge, which can be used to develop an even better future generation of the product.

It is essential to note that it is *product research* that is almost ignored. Detailed product research slows up the introduction process, as it takes time to implement and analyse. The 'real' marketplace gives 'real' information, which makes it a more precise indicator than research reports. While in principle such an entrepreneurial approach is a very good idea, it can only work if it is set on a very solid foundation of customer knowledge, otherwise costly mistakes are easily made. A thorough understanding of the customers' probable interests and habits – together with a lot of experience of turning the prime movers in the marketplace into customers – are essential factors in applying these methods.

The Benihana restaurant chain is a rather unorthodox example to illustrate the importance of understanding the customer and doing *customer* research properly and thoroughly. In 1964 a new Japanese restaurant concept was launched in mid-town Manhattan. It grew from nothing to reach a $12 million turnover with 15 units within seven years. The name of the chain was Benihana, the founder Hiroaki (Rocky) Aoki. Rocky Aoki was not a newcomer to the restaurant business. He came from a family of restaurateurs in Japan, but he had no experience of the US at the time of starting his project. The concept Rocky Aoki created and introduced was to offer the American steakhouse restaurant customers exotic meals, prepared in front of their eyes in an entertaining way by Japanese master chefs, with the whole setting being fairly informal. The founder personally spent not months but three years studying the American market before he launched his concept. He spent time observing the environment, talking to people, going to restaurants to study his future competitors, studying the economics of running a restaurant in the US, etc. His formula, 'concept', although Japanese at heart, was skilfully adapted to US restaurant habits and had immediate great appeal. To ensure a commercial success, the restaurants were designed so that the profitability of each visitor was maximized. The customer-flow ensured that enough time was given to pre-dinner drinks (very profitable) while as little time as possible was spent on keeping restaurant seats occupied. The seating arrangement ('bartype') ensured a high customer density and the chef provided not only the food but, more importantly, the entertainment value. The concept was a great success and, a large part of the reason for the success was undoubtedly that, by doing his homework so thoroughly, the founder truly understood his customers.

A very different story, but one with a similar basic message that it is essential to understand the customers, comes from the world of consumer electronics. In this case, the 'understanding' was used to see how the then modern (and in some respects yet-to-be-invented) technology could make a known product into a more interesting product for a much wider audience. Not niche marketing, but rather the reverse – transforming a niche product into a mass market product. The example relates to the enormous market for video recorders.

The first commercially available video recorder came on the market in 1954, and was American. It was also very big and expensive, and the only people who could afford to buy it and use it were television companies. They loved it because it made it possible to tape shows rather than having to broadcast 'live'. The company, Ampex, logically focused its efforts on producing a definite video recorder for the studio market. For instance, they improved to perfection the machine's ability to play back pre-recorded sequences – a key feature for the studio market. After a couple of years, Ampex was quite content with its position as a strong market leader in a 'nice' niche.

The Japanese companies looked at the market differently. They realized that such a machine would have a great value in the home, and there were many more homes than television studios. But they also understood that with a new customer group the technical specifications could be quite different. On the one hand, the size of the machine had to be smaller to fit into a home environment and it had to be much easier to use. The Ampex machines were big and were designed to be operated by skilled engineers, using a bulky two-inch tape. On the other hand, the general picture quality and the precision in starting and stopping could be of a lower standard as home viewing is technically less demanding than studio recordings.

Sony came up with the technical solution and the Japanese companies now dominate the huge global market for VCRs. Sony designed the VHS cassette, making the handling of the tape a simple matter compared to an open-reel system, and as Sony had tilted the recording head a narrower ¾-inch tape could be used, thus reducing the size of the machine. As the home user market cannot utilize studio standards, the lower technical quality was not a real disadvantage, especially seen in the light of the significantly improved ease-of-handling. The Japanese understood that a 'normal' consumer has different values to those of a professional studio manager. Sony had the vision to conceptualize that the video recorder could be something for the consumer market, and they had the spirit to carry through the project. Market research and market segmentation studies would have been of little help; creative understanding of consumer value was of fundamental importance.

In a general sense the end result of the Japanese phenomenon is very basic: they offer a better product at a competitive price. There was nothing magic about the Japanese attack on the motorcycle market in the 1960s, which wiped out the vast majority of US and European manufacturers. The Japanese motorbike was just a more appealing product. It represented good value, it was exciting and it made motorbikes fashionable (again). Also, the cars from Japan were certainly not the types of vehicles, at least not in the early days, that one would dream about. However, they offered excellent value for money with fundamental consumer benefits, reliability and economy, and with the basic engineering well executed. The ability of the Japanese to do so rested on superior production technology. The marketing result was that the customers received a reliable and generally attractive product when they bought a Japanese car. In a classical marketing sense there was very little that was new, the only new thing was that the products offered significantly better value for money!

Conclusion

The examples from the Japanese wave show that one has constantly to search for product improvements to make the products, or the services, better value. That search has to be based on solid consumer knowledge, otherwise the work will be in vain.

There are many other examples of successful businesses that one could mention with European or American origins, such as the German car manufacturers Mercedes-Benz and BMW, or the UK retailers Marks & Spencer and J Sainsbury's. I have focused on the examples from Japan, because they have been the most successful in gaining market share over the last 20 years. The current and potential losers of market share have to become more aggressive to combat these continuing attacks. In sectors where the Japanese wave has not yet arrived, other companies from other countries are busy enhancing their product ranges.

For a successful, competitive strategy it is essential to learn the lessons and improve the products so that it will be possible to compete and survive in the future marketing battles.

5

Attraction and over-satisfaction

The marketing literature is full of definitions of new terms and concepts. Just like many other social sciences, various authors have over the years invented new expressions. In my approach to marketing I have deliberately avoided too many new expressions. Nevertheless, a few are necessary to describe and discuss the essential understanding of the consumers' purchasing process and the various factors that influence that process. The terminology is a part of the methodology.

Perceived value

The most important factor influencing the purchasing process is the *perceived value*. For a customer in a potential purchasing situation the fact that will influence him or her to buy or not to buy is the perception of the product on offer.

A product's perceived value is not constant; it varies with each customer and can even change according to the time of the day or the year. A swim-suit, for example, does not have a very high perceived value in the middle of winter, unless you are going on holiday to a warm climate.

Perceived value = The customer's impression of a product's benefits

The perceived value is different from the objective value because it is the emotional impression of an individual, a human being. It is not something that the customer arrives at in an objective or logical way.

In theory, purchasing decisions are supposed to be the result of a factual comparison of the benefits of buying a specific product and other ways of spending the money. In reality the decisions are based on the perceived value and that value is, by definition, biased one way or another, making the whole purchasing process subjective, not objective. In FMCG, in particular, that subjectivity is inflated by the superficial way the customers reach their decisions. Owing to pressure of time, they are unlikely to take all aspects of the perceived value into account when they do their weekly shopping.

When planning a marketing programme, it is essential to bear in mind that it is only the perceived value that will influence the customer, not the 'cost' value. As all experienced business people know, it does not matter how well a product is made or how ingeniously it is designed if those values are not appreciated or even recognized by the customer. The perceived value, from the customer's viewpoint, is in no way related to the cost of manufacturing. The value is only related to the customer's perception of the dimensions that are relevant to him or her. (There are of course exceptions to this in the luxury market. The very fact that something is expensive to make gives a specific product a high perceived value in certain instances.) On the other hand, despite this emphasis on the subjective perceived value, it is equally essential to realize that if a perceived value is to be credible it must be based on real, factual product properties. I shall elaborate on this aspect later in the book.

The dismal success rate of new products is evidence of the difficulties of correctly evaluating the perceived value. By definition, the decision to launch a product that later fails is a misjudgement of the perceived value. If the perceived value for money of a product is higher than that of the competition, it will sell; if not, it will not sell. Since approximately 70 per cent of the new FMCG products (Chapter 2) that are launched do not survive, the ability to judge the perceived value for money in the FMCG industry is low. More emphasis needs to be given to the evaluation of the perceived value for money of new products. It is possible that less products would be launched, but the success rate would certainly be much higher.

It is a comforting thought, but in my view not an excuse, that there are many well-known examples of how otherwise skilled business people have misjudged the perceived value of their 'pet projects'. Spectacular illustrations are Clive Sinclair's C5 vehicle, the late Robert Maxwell's 24-hour London newspaper and, of course – as no marketing book is complete without a reference to it – the Ford Edsel. (The Ford Edsel was created in the late 1950s to 'fill a gap' in the Ford range of automobiles in the US. It failed not only because similar cars were already available, but more importantly because the market switched away from the big gas-guzzlers to smaller cars. Ford lost $350 million.)

In order to be able to develop the sales of a product range it is essential to understand the relevance of the perceived value, especially in contrast to the cost of manufacturing. The term 'perceived value' is at the very heart of the modern approach to marketing.

Initial and repeat purchases

There are basically two types of purchases: *initial* purchases and *repeat* purchases. From a marketing viewpoint, the main difference between the two is that one is made on the basis of real experience and the other on the basis of a perception.

A customer, when making an initial purchase, has no actual experience of the product at the moment of making the decision. The customer has never used it and his or her perceived value of the product is a result of only what has been seen or heard.

The repeat purchase (or sale if seen from the producer), on the other hand, is based on, or at least heavily influenced by, previous own experience of the product. Consequently, the customer's memory of using the product plays an important part in his or her assessment of the perceived value when deliberating over a potential repeat purchase.

By dividing the sales of a product into these two categories, one gets a better grasp of where the potential for sales improvement lies, as well as a better understanding of how sales have grown in the past.

If a business is to grow it must generate new customers faster than old ones disappear, i.e. increase the penetration, or increase the repeat purchase rate. Using a wide definition, the latter can be achieved not only by increasing the conversion rate of initial purchases but also by making each customer buy more often, or buy more each time.

Neither of the two types of purchases can be ignored, but, for future prosperity in a very competitive climate, the ability to generate repeat business is the more important.

Attraction

An initial purchase is influenced by factors quite different from those needed to achieve a high repeat purchase rate. The number of customers of a product, the penetration, is determined by the ability of a product to *communicate* attractive perceived value for money. One product is preferable to another because it has greater *attraction* values. The greater the attraction, the higher the penetration.

Attraction = Pre-purchase perceived value for money

For most products the initial purchases form a small part of the total sales; the repeat business from the heavy users is much more important. The ability to generate new customers cannot be ignored; even a healthy business needs to replace lapsed buyers.

To gain more trials, more customers must feel that the product on offer gives them a better value for their resources than the alternatives. The marketer has to create this impression without the customer using the product. It is, in effect, totally dependent on communication but there are many different ways in which an improved attraction can be achieved, such as a new advertising campaign, a revised pack design or perhaps a word-of-mouth campaign.

It is also feasible that the attraction will improve in relative terms rather than in absolute terms. If one competitor disappears, there are less available alternatives, so the remaining ones become relatively stronger. It is also possible that, for some reason, a competing product becomes less attractive. Again the remaining ones will gain in relative perceived attraction. These two last situations are mentioned more from a theoretical than a practical point of view. It is much more likely that the competitive products will *improve* their attraction values.

The behaviour of street traders provides a simplistic example of creating attraction. They do not have the marketing tools of a big company, but they can use their products to create 'sales appeal'. Their customers are attracted by the visual impact they create on their stands, for instance the display of vegetables or flowers, as well as by the way they shout out the virtues of their goods. Skilled traders know how to display their wares so that the maximum impact is created. Their produce is shown at its best, not over-promising as that will rebound, but treading the careful line between credibility and over-persuasive sales talk.

A fairly detailed analysis of how a first purchase is made, as the one in the preceding paragraphs, can create the impression that the decision to make an initial purchase is well-considered. As most marketers know, the decision to try a new FMCG product is usually instantaneous. When exposed to a new pack in the supermarket, the decision is made within minutes, if not seconds, based on a positive attitude to the product's perceived value.

There are, of course, exceptions to the general rule. For instance, the first pack of baby food a first-time mother buys is often the result of a very carefully made decision. Also, if a consumer has a particular interest, such as slimming or health food, such a purchase will be well considered.

A personal survey of purchases in a supermarket on a Friday afternoon will give convincing examples of irrational and rapid decision making. The modern man or woman has simply not enough time to make rational decisions each time a purchase is made. Also, many purchases represent such a low outlay that any time-consuming deliberate analysis is just not worth the customer's effort. It is easier and quicker to experiment and try a product as long as the overall proposition seems reasonable.

Despite this sometimes irrational behaviour it is important to note that each decision, each purchase made, represents a choice – a choice of making a specific purchase or using the money for something else. The choice that is made may be very undiscerning and may be made without much deliberation, but it is made and the determining factor is the perceived value for money that has been created for the product.

The attraction is based on the perceived pre-purchase or pre-consumption/usage value. In order to have a strong new business position in the marketplace, a company must constantly build the attraction of the products. The attraction can be created in many different ways, depending on the type of product, purchasing pattern, tradition, etc. The challenge for the marketer is to ensure that the product at the point of sale is perceived as the superior one and thus will be the one that is chosen.

Over-satisfaction

In the building of a business, or when a new product is being launched, the pre-purchase attraction of the product will determine whether it will be a success or not. As soon as the introduction phase is over, the *repeat business* takes priority. In the total business environment it is only a small proportion of all products that are in the introduction phase. By far the vast majority is existing business, with existing products and services, where the key to success is a high repeat purchase rate. For example, let us consider a gardener: it is important to plant and sow, but it is even more important to ensure that the plants grow by nurturing them, otherwise there will be no produce to enjoy. It is the nurturing of a product range that will create a good repeat business rate.

Repeat business is important for a number of reasons; the most important being that if there is no repeat business, the customer base will expire. It does not matter how good the attraction might be – there will soon be no more customers to attract. Another reason is that repeat business is more profitable. It is easier to sell to someone who has already been a customer than to search for new customers. The cost of the expensive 'recruitment' of customers can be spread across a greater sales volume, compared to the situation with a non-repeat buyer where the full cost will have to be carried by the sale of just one product.

Experience backs these arguments for high repeat purchase rates. If a FMCG product or business is to be successful, it must have a minimum initial repeat purchase rate of 50–70 per cent, otherwise the cost of generating new customers in relation to the existing ones becomes too high.

Obviously all companies would like to have products with a repeat purchase rate of 100 per cent, but unfortunately this seldom occurs, for several reasons. The most basic reason is that it is improbable that everyone who tries a product will like it to the extent of wanting to buy it again. Another is that, in many product categories, the cost of changing and trying something new is fairly low. It does not cost much, nor does it represent a great risk, to try a different brand of margarine or a different brand of marmalade. In other product categories there is a great demand for variety, such as in prepared ready meals or yogurts. As it can be difficult for one brand to carry a range that will give sufficient choice, there is consequently quite an amount of brand switching. In this latter case, the repeat purchase rate in the sense of brand loyalty can still be quite high as the customers will eventually come back to the favourites.

One has to be careful of how the repeat purchase rate is estimated. Depending on the category, the rate can be the absolute number based on actual purchase, or it can be the intention to buy again. The first instance would represent a capital good, such as a car; the second, a low-priced grocery item, such as a pack of fish fingers.

The intention to make a repeat purchase grows out of the experience the customer has had of the usage of the product plus any communication to which the customer has been exposed. Based on those experiences the product has accumulated a perceived value in the mind of the customer. If the appeal of that value is stronger than that of the alternatives, then the customer will *prefer* that product. It has achieved a preference over similar products or even over an alternative use of the money.

It is obvious that to become the preferred product the use of the product must be a positive experience. The old saying that the proof of the pudding lies in the eating is applicable also to marketing!

The customer must feel truly satisfied when using the product. Such a positive customer satisfaction can only come out of a positive product or service experience. That positive feeling has its foundation in a perception that the product has fulfilled the requirements the customer set when making the original purchase. In other words, the perceived value the customer felt the product had at the point of purchase, must also be delivered at the moment of usage.

There is also a negative side to this argument: after an unsatisfactory experience the customer will certainly not come back.

While it is easy to talk and write about high repeat purchase rates, achieving them can be quite difficult. Let us use the simple example of a street market. A greengrocer will ensure good repeat business by having good quality products (= fresh produce), honest communication (= no over-ripe produce at the bottom of the bag), a good range of products and reasonable prices. A friendly face and the skill to recognize customers as they come back adds extra value to the produce. So even in the fairly uncomplicated marketing world of a greengrocer, the factors that make up the repeat purchase rate are quite complex. In principle, this consists of two parts: the experience of actually using the product and the communication that surrounds the purchase and the usage. Both factors are important in achieving a positive impression of the actual usage of the product.

If a product is just, in classical terms, fulfilling a need or a want, the repeat purchase rate is vulnerable. It is only by having a result that *exceeds* the alternatives beyond the satisfaction of the 'needs' that the marketer's mission is achieved. The product must achieve *over-satisfaction*.

Over-satisfaction = Superior experience-based perceived value for money

The importance of maintaining customer satisfaction and an excellent perceived value over time was proved in a survey, made by AC Nielsen Research Company for the *Checkout* magazine in December 1989, of the top grocery brands in the UK. One of the conclusions was that the average age of the top 10 packaged grocery brands in the UK in 1989 was 42 years. (The brands ranked 11–20 had an average age of 49 years.) The youngest brand, Flora, was launched in 1964; the oldest, Heinz Baked Beans, was brought to the UK in 1901. All the top 10 brands (Persil detergents, Nescafé coffee, Whiskas cat food, Ariel detergents, Andrex toilet paper, Coca-Cola, PG Tips tea, Pedigree Chum dog food, Heinz Baked Beans and Flora margarine) have a history of careful and committed brand management. The products that carry these brands have continuously been upgraded and modified to follow the trends of the environment. Despite their considerable age the brands are not seen as old fashioned.

As further proof of the importance of existing brands, and how it is possible to nurture old products into several decades of growth, only three of the top 50 brands in the Nielsen survey were launched after 1980 (Kleenex toilet tissue, Clover spread and St Ivel Shape yogurt).

Another survey, by the design consultants Landor, covering the top 10 brands of the total UK business scene (published in the *Marketing* magazine), gave results consistent with the Nielsen analysis. The brands, Marks & Spencer, Cadbury, Kellogg, Heinz, Rolls-Royce, Boots, Nescafé, BBC, Rowntree and J Sainsbury's, are all old but are perceived as contemporary. They are also brands that stand for quality and/or superior service. They are the kind of values that have a timeless quality and represent factors that have a great impact on perceived value.

Products really need to be taken care of. One way of looking at this is to compare the product (or the brand) of a company with a fixed installation, such as a machine. If the machine is to maintain its ability to produce, it must be maintained. It must be looked after; the old and worn parts must be replaced and it sometimes needs a complete overhaul to ensure that it is working properly. All through its life it must be serviced, oil added, bolts adjusted, etc. If it is neglected over a long period, it will probably have to be scrapped.

Lack of machine maintenance means capital degeneration. With a product it is similarly a question of maintenance. The product needs to be looked after, modified as society changes, adapted and developed, but never neglected. By continuously working with the product and improving it, the quality is enhanced and the perceived value remains on top.

A different example of successfully building repeat business is the Volvo Car Company in its home market, Sweden. The company's success over the years has been based on a determined policy of ensuring that the repeat purchase rate is high. Over the last 40 years, it has always been the best in the car industry, often up to 80 per cent, which is very difficult to achieve and maintain in such a competitive and changing market.

The factors behind this solid and long-term success are many. In the car business, as in all other businesses, the repeat purchase rate depends on the *total* experience of owning the car such as quality, service, spare parts, etc. One of the major factors in Volvo's success is the dealer network. The truly national organization is made up of franchised, independent dealers (60 per cent) and a network of agencies owned by a separate, Volvo controlled public company. The dealers provide a service of a very high standard, and it has been proved that the repeat purchase rate is strongly influenced by the availability of first-class service garages. The management of the dealer network makes sure that staff training is well in advance of competition and that the Volvo mechanic-manuals and the service programmes are far superior to competition in its detail and comprehensiveness. All elements are constantly upgraded to ensure that Volvo keeps its leadership.

Another factor is that, over the last 40–50 years, the policy of the dealer network has been to ensure that the second-hand value of the cars is maintained at a relatively high level. The purchaser of a Volvo car is assured of receiving a reasonable price for the car when it is due for replacement. This makes the customer more likely to visit a Volvo dealer when a change of car is considered, as the Volvo dealer is concerned to keep the value up and will offer as good a price, if not better, than anyone else.

To further improve the perceived and real value of owning a Volvo the dealers can offer advantageous financing through Volvo (Volvofinans) and attractive insurance through Volvo's insurance company (Volvia). Also, a Volvo credit card permits the owners to buy petrol and certain other items more cheaply. Volvo takes a total view of the car ownership and uses all possible routes to give the Volvo owner superb value so that the repeat purchase is ensured. The end result of these strategies, in combination with a basically well-engineered and long-lasting car, is that the brand share has been kept at a very high level, approximately 30 per cent, despite a premium priced product. What, perhaps, is even more important is that the company and its retailers, the Volvo distributors, are historically very profitable.

The repeat purchase rate is the key factor in having a successful and profitable business. The customer will only be loyal to a brand and a product for as long as it offers better perceived value for money than alternative products. To ensure that a company will keep its customers it has to deliver a product that not only satisfies certain needs but gives over-satisfaction. Many products can fulfil a need, but only one can be superior.

Conclusion

The perceived value is the crucial factor that will determine whether a customer will buy a product initially, and then again. The initial purchase is dependent on the attraction the manufacturer can generate; the repeat purchase depends on the ability of the product to deliver over-satisfaction, to achieve a preference with the customer. Only by having a product with a strong customer preference, generating repeat business, can a company be sure of a successful future.

6

Value-added marketing: the new concept

Marketing needs to regain the competitive edge it has lost in an accelerating way over the last 20 years. North American and western European FMCG industries have failed to maintain the momentum that classical marketing gave them in the 1950s and the 1960s. In particular, the industries of the USA and the UK have seen their world brand share deteriorate over time, despite (or perhaps because of) a conscientious application of classical marketing theory.

In contrast to the major western FMCG companies, the competitors – in particular, Japanese companies, but also some quality conscious western companies – have pursued a strategy of rapid and dedicated product improvement. Existing products are constantly improved and the new products that are launched offer better value for money. This is achieved through higher specifications or lower prices, or both.

In the west, some very successful UK retailers, such as Tesco, J Sainsbury's and Marks & Spencer, have with great thrust pushed their quality levels well beyond those of 10 years ago. Conventional wisdom among FMCG marketers used to be that the consumers were not willing to pay a premium for a higher quality product, but the retail scene of the 1980s and the early 1990s has proved that theory to be wrong.

To maintain and expand a FMCG business in the future will put even greater demands on the skills that are needed to persuade the customers to choose a particular product. The total grocery market is virtually static and very few product segments experience any growth. As a basic strategy, all FMCG companies will have to protect their existing sales against competitors and retailers' own labels. The progressive strategic option is to develop their market share, at the expense of either competitive manufacturers or competitive product groups. In an overall static market that is much more likely to lead to increased sales and profits than trying to define and exploit new market segments. Today there are very few unfulfilled consumer needs that the FMCG marketer can exploit. The consumers are much more interested in products of a higher quality than in new products.

In both strategies marketers must ensure, first, that their products are more attractive to the customers and, second, that they deliver over-satisfaction. That is the only way to achieve the repeat purchase and penetration rates that will make it possible to retain a market position and increase sales.

The marketing profession has the potential to play an important role in the battle for market share, but to do so it has to change. A new marketing concept is needed. The marketing man or woman of today is following principles which, over the last decade, have proved to be inefficient. Conscientiously following the track of fulfilling needs has not brought the success that marketers or their directors expected. Their skills have been wasted. It is difficult to imagine how many marketing man-hours lie behind all failed new product launches, but consider the following. An estimated minimum of 12 000 new food products are launched each year in western Europe and the USA. If one disregards all the projects that never made it to launch, and if we assume (a) a 70 per cent failure rate and (b) that there is one year's work behind each, then we can conclude that 8400 working years have been wasted! That is in food products only. No one is motivated by failure, and a higher success rate would do wonders for the marketers' esteem in their own eyes as well as in others.

My message is that, for the 1990s, marketing needs to move ahead to a new level. Classical marketing has not moved with the times and has not changed sufficiently to be effective in the 1990s. Despite this, one has to realize that the underlying philosophy is timeless; that is, you must please your customer if you are to remain in business. After all traders have always known that you must keep the customer satisfied!

My new concept is based on the assumption that the marketers already know and can use classical marketing. There are situations in which classical marketing is applicable (as was shown in the case of Timotei), but in many other situations marketing practitioners need to change their approach.

The concept

In redefining and improving marketing I have two *objectives*:

1 to give the marketing profession a new direction for the application of its skills

2 to give the traditional marketing-led companies an approach that will enable them to compete successfully with entrepreneurial and quality-focused organizations.

The need for marketing-led companies to improve their success rate is obvious from the arguments already presented. The entrepreneurs were much admired during the 1980s, but renewed marketing-led companies have the opportunity to fight back in the 1990s. This can be done if marketing executives follow updated principles.

The role of marketing in the future should be

> **TO CONSTANTLY IMPROVE THE PERCEIVED RELATIVE VALUE FOR MONEY OF THE COMPANY'S PRODUCTS**

The marketing executive can achieve this by focusing on

> **VALUE MAXIMIZATION**

I have called this principle *value-added marketing*. It is based on the obvious but often disregarded fact that to gain market share you have to offer products that are superior to those that are already available.

If a company adopts value-added marketing it will become more prosperous. Value-added marketing will create higher attraction and over-satisfaction values for the company's products, thus giving higher customer penetration and, more importantly, superior repeat purchase rates. That, in itself, is enough to improve the operation's efficiencies but, as I shall show later, the new marketing concept will also give the company other direct and indirect benefits, all contributing towards making the company more profitable.

Value-added marketing brings a new dimension to marketing, removing it from the search for empty niches in the market place and giving it a determined strategy of improving the perception of existing products, adding new ones only when a significant benefit is to be gained.

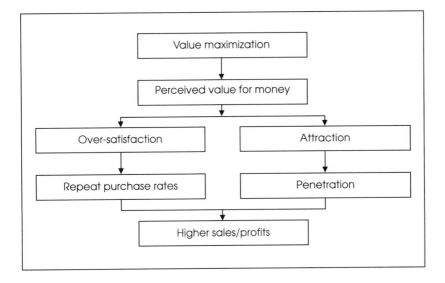

Figure 6.1 The value-added marketing process

This new mode of operation will make the marketer strive constantly towards perfection in all aspects of the marketing mix. From the core tasks of making the use of the product a more pleasant and rewarding experience to ensuring that the aura of the product transmits strong positive values. Many successful companies of today are already instinctively following this quest for a 'better world' of products, but in this book I shall present a framework of how to apply it (Figure 6.1).

Key expressions

To clarify the concept in more detail, I have below elaborated on the key words and, where appropriate, compared them with classical marketing procedures.

Constantly   Value-added marketing requires constant attention of the marketers. One of the more common reasons for the demise of many products is that they are not adapted to the changing habits and attitudes of the customers. Similarly, one of the key factors behind long-term successful products and brands is constant innovation, adaptation and improvement. The retail trade offers an interesting example. The range of a retailer is his or her 'product', and it is constantly reviewed. It is impossible for a retailer to survive without changing and improving the range. Why, then, should a FMCG company be able to survive without improving its products?

In order to be successful the task must never be considered finished. The products must be reviewed and improved constantly as both customers and competition continue to change. Only if all competitors and customers decide to stop changing can a company stop adapting and modifying its product range. Value-added marketing is not the same as classical marketing, where the project is finished once the market segment is identified and the product launched.

Improve   Everything can always be done better, is a basic axiom of value-added marketing. The necessity of constantly improving the products is relevant both to new products and to existing ones. Existing products have to be made better, and new products must represent a substantial improvement on any alternatives already on the market. What to improve will be dealt with later. The improvement philosophy is crucial to the survival of any business; it is only by staying ahead that market shares can be defended and/or expanded. For a practitioner of classical marketing, the objective is to get as close as possible to fulfilling a specific need. Value-added marketing's improvement philosophy means that you have to aim for and achieve over-satisfaction; you must go beyond the need-fulfilment to ensure that the perception of the product on offer exceeds the alternatives. It also has to be said that 'improvement' refers to all elements in the product mix, from quality to communication and from selling price to press release.

Perceived   The term 'perceived value', explained earlier, is of fundamental importance. The perception of a product at the point of potential purchase needs to be made as positive as possible. This perception forms the basis of the customer's decision to buy or not to buy.

Relative   The perceived value is a subjective statement, not an absolute fact. The value/price relation of an item is not evaluated only in relation to the product group but to the whole of the customer's product universe. A specific product might be quite competitive within its product category, but if the total category is losing its competitiveness, the long-term future will be gloomy. To be successful the marketer must adapt the customer's way of looking at the values of the products. That is why the *relative* value is used in the concept definition.

Value   A customer sees a number of benefits or values in a product. These add up to a total impression of the product's value. A product has, for each customer in principle, a unique set of benefits. In reality the basic benefits or values are fairly consistent across the population. It is not that everyone thinks alike, but core values are often universal. It is important to have a distinct view of how the customers evaluate the products' benefits, as it is impossible to improve something that is neither known nor reasonably well defined. Of course, what a product is worth objectively, based on the manufacturing costs, is of no relevance.

Money   The perceived relative value is seen in the context of what it costs to acquire: i.e. money. The cost of a product creates the cut-off point for a customer. If something is given away free, or for very little, many people would like to have it; and the more expensive, the less demand. That, at least, is the theory although there are many exceptions. The marketer can influence the value-for-money balance by creating value and by reducing the perceived cost.

Product   The following is more for the record. Although the word 'product' has been used in the text, everything that is said regarding products applies equally to 'services'. There is one point worth mentioning in this context, i.e. the customer buys a product (or service), not a brand or an image. The action, the decision to buy and part with money, refers to a product. This will be discussed further in Chapter 15.

Value maximization   The day-to-day objective for the marketer is to aim for value maximization, obviously within the relevant cost parameters. The only exception to the necessity of dealing with a comparative value as opposed to an absolute, is where the potential customer has unlimited funds – a highly unlikely event! In theory, it is sufficient that a product is 'just' better than its competition because the customer evaluates on a relative basis, i.e. compares one product with another, and makes a decision. In reality, in virtually all cases the competitive situation is such that the different value-dimensions need to be pushed to the limit to ensure that the company's products will continue to sell.

All through the elaborations on the value-added marketing principles I have emphasized the relative perceived value as being opposite to objective, 'real' values. As a paragraph of caution I would like to add the following. It is tempting to place too much emphasis on the more glamorous intangible values, such as creating an attractive and exciting image. It is very important to be aware of the significance of the 'hard' values that go with a product such as quality, reliability, consistency, etc. Just as the imagery reflects on and enhances the 'real' value, the reverse is certainly also true. It is almost impossible to have a product with a high perceived value without an objectively real value substance. In their best-selling business book, *In Search of Excellence*, Peters and Waterman described a number of successful companies, one of which was

Procter and Gamble. The point that was mentioned most frequently to Peters and Waterman in their interviews regarding P&G, was product quality. P&G, who are renowned for their (classical) marketing skills, are obsessed with quality, and rightly so. Also, in the world of household products, where product quality is sometimes disregarded, P&G have realized that it pays to be beset by quality.

Conclusion

The application of value-added marketing will make any company's product range more competitive. The focus on achieving over-satisfaction and greater attraction through value maximization will result in an increase in the perceived 'value for money'.

A new concept is not useful unless it can be used in an effective way, which is why I shall explain in the remainder of the book how the marketing executive can use this new approach. Value-added marketing will make the company stronger and marketing more relevant for the world of tomorrow.

7

The value balance

The first step in the process of value-added marketing is to establish the current situation with regard to the perceived values of the various products, brands or ranges. It is like building a house; before you erect the walls, you ensure that the foundation is solid, and before building the foundation, you ensure that you are building on the right plot.

The usefulness of any evaluation is obviously dependent on its accuracy. The need for at least a certain amount of objectivity can create some problems for a brand manager who, almost every day, is 'selling' his or her products internally to other departments. It is easy to fall into the trap of looking at a product in a more positive light than the real situation justifies. The problem should not be over-stated, but one has to be aware of the incompatibility of a dedicated entrepreneur and an unemotional analyst. It is probably better for a company to have a dedicated, committed marketer who is a less objective analyst, than the reverse. One also has to consider that an over-enthusiastic bias will only make the analysis less reliable in comparisons with the competition. The part of the analysis that covers the definition of the most important dimensions is, in principle, unaffected as the enthusiasm is unlikely to influence the selection and ranking of these variables to any significant degree.

As the first step in the implementation process, it is necessary to clarify the status of the company's products in the minds of the customers: What is the value balance?

The perceived value of each and every product that is being sold consists of tangible and intangible values. The customers set the total 'sum' of these values against the perceived cost of the product, as shown in Figure 7.1. These values can be both generic core values and supplementary brand specific ones.

How the value balance tilts determines whether a product is bought or not. The various values aggregate to a total that is judged in

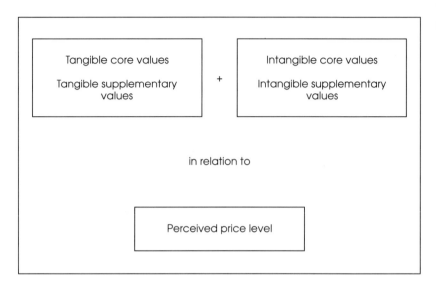

Figure 7.1 The value balance

relation to the perceived cost. If the values outweigh the cost, the product is bought; if the perceived cost outweighs the values, the product is not bought.

The stronger the perceived value in relation to cost, the larger the market share (Figure 7.2).

The selection of what product to buy in the FMCG market is theoretically a two-stage process. The first stage is a selection of what CATEGORY of product to buy, say fish fingers or instant coffee; the second stage is what BRAND or pack of fish fingers or coffee to buy. In both instances the choice is made on the basis of the outcome of the value balance. The product with the most advantageous value balance will be bought. For the analytical process it can be sensible to bear the two stages in mind as that will explain why, in a product sector, an alternative that is ranked second and has a very positive value balance still does not get chosen. The primary choice will have had an even better balance and the customer is only interested in buying one product of that kind. In the day-to-day work the two-stage analysis has only limited use as the objective for the marketer is always to maximize the value side of the balance.

The establishment of the value balance is a three-step process. The first step is to DEFINE the variables that make up the balance. The second step is to establish the PRIORITY RANKING of the various variables, how do the various variables rank in importance with the

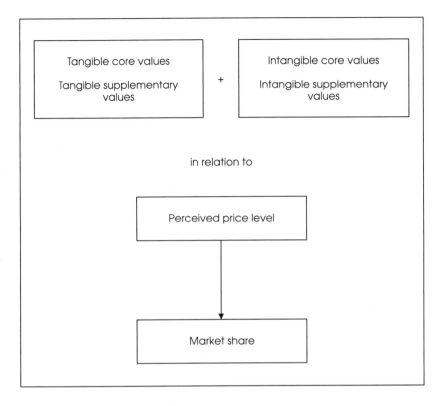

Figure 7.2 The effect of the value balance

customer. The third step is to evaluate the COMPETITIVE STRENGTH of the different variables of the product.

The process of defining the key dimensions

In order to start to build the knowledge of how the customers see the perceived values of a product, one needs to define the main dimensions, i.e. the dimensions that make people buy the product. We can illustrate this with an example from the food area, such as baked beans. What are the reasons behind a customer's choice of category of product and a specific brand? Does the customer buy the beans because they just taste good, or is it perhaps because the tomato sauce has the right balance of sweetness and acidity and that the beans are cooked to the correct softness? Is it because baked beans are a cheap way of filling up the children's empty stomachs, or is it perhaps that baked beans are extremely convenient to prepare (you just have to open the can and heat them), or is it perhaps that the brand in question features a particular healthy type of baked beans? Or, as a final alternative, is it that the brand is the one that the family has learned to trust over many years? In any event, the choice is a mix of category and brand and is certain to include several variables, rather than one. Fortunately from the marketer's point of view it is also likely that, for each individual customer, there are probably only two to four main variables that will account for the greater part of the purchasing decision.

If for each customer one has to take into account two to four variables, one can conclude that six or seven variables will cover the great majority of the perceived values that will influence the purchasing decisions of the target group. At least in the FMCG markets, the key factors making up the total perceived value are rarely more than seven. The overall heavy information flow and the relatively minor importance given to a FMCG purchase do not, in general, allow for a more complex mix of values to penetrate to the customer.

While the number of dimensions might well be small, their make-up can easily make the matter more complicated. This latter point opens up the possibilities for improvement: there is very little scope for value enhancement in a simple, uncomplicated dimension such as the size of the baked beans tin (bigger or smaller), but a more complex dimension such as 'flavour' or 'authenticity' opens up several opportunities and directions. With a good understanding of the totality of these value-giving dimensions, the marketer can select the most opportune way to improve the perceived value of a product and, consequently, increase sales.

The second aspect of the analysis is that there is, of course, a hierarchy or priority ranking of the various product values in the minds of the customers, i.e. what a customer regards as important or less important for the product group as a whole and for the specific brands. Is the type of beans in the baked beans tin important? Is the type of fish in the fish finger a relevant factor? Are these the factors that will make the customer buy or not? The analysis and listing of the dimensions that create the perceived product values must be done in the context of the importance the customers set on them. It is not the relevant dimensions from a *manufacturing* point of view that should be listed, regardless of how fascinating they are; it is what the *customers* see as giving the perceived values that determines the importance of any specific dimension.

After defining and ranking the dimensions that create the total perceived value of a product, the third step is to evaluate them. Obviously the evaluation has to be done as objectively as possible. It is unavoidable that the procedure will be subjective to a certain degree, as it involves personal judgements, but the marketer must try to minimize the subjectivity. It is impossible to be totally objective; it is not even a guarantee to rely on market research as that is just someone else's subjectivity. A well-founded evaluation, with the ambition to be as accurate as possible, is probably the best method of getting the value dimensions charted.

The evaluation can be made in absolute terms or in relation to competitive products. The latter method is most often easier, and the perceived *relative* value is the most relevant parameter when defining the requirements for future improvement.

At its first introduction, this whole exercise is a fairly large undertaking as it involves getting to know not only the company's own products but also the customers and the competition in some detail. At the second review, and the essential updates, it is much easier as the groundwork has already been done.

The process of establishing the value balance is important in order to get a full understanding of the perceived values. For the enhancement activity that will follow, it is almost imperative that the current situation is clarified prior to the start of any extensive work on improving the perceived position, otherwise – continuing the analogue of house building – the building work might be started on the wrong plot or without a solid foundation.

When changing a company's working methods to make it more efficient, it is a common attitude to take the view that most of what has been done in the past is, at best, poor-quality workmanship. Even if that is true, provided that a company is generating *some* sales, then someone, somewhere, must be perceiving the products as giving a positive value experience. In reality, in most cases a considerable number of positive perceived values are tied to a company's products. Obviously, one has to realize what those values are so that they can be retained for future use. One also has to appreciate the context within which they generate a positive perception. A product can be selling, not because of the product's own values but, for instance, because of a very strong presence in the distribution channels. Alternatively, the product might be selling on the back of other well-regarded products from the same company. This complex of finding the values that really are important is essential to an understanding of how the total perceived value of a product is generated. The broader picture will also give important indications of all those areas in which it is possible to enhance the value of the product.

Table 7.1 Key dimensions (fictitious example)

Variable

Tangible
Core values
  Taste
  Convenience
  Filling
Supplementary values
  Versatile
  Healthy

Intangible
Core values
  Popular
  Traditional
Supplementary values
  Children's favourite
  Exciting to eat

Perceived price

The establishment of the value balance is the first step on the road to applying, and receiving benefits from, value-added marketing. The balance consists of two parts: firstly, the perceived value of the product (i.e. what the customer gets) and, secondly, the price of the product (i.e. what the customer pays).

The value side of the balance

The more complex part of the value balance is the *value side*. Although the price of a product is not such a simple one-dimensional matter as one might think, the value side is by far the more complicated as the perceived value of a product can be made up of many more different dimensions than the price.

The value-giving dimensions have to be clearly defined and understood. A daunting task, perhaps, but as only a small number of dimensions are relevant, it is no more complicated than a standard segmentation analysis.

The first step is to establish a list of the key dimensions under each main heading, as shown in Table 7.1.

A totally fictitious baked beans example is used to illustrate how one can start a value balance analysis. The various dimensions are listed in two groups, tangible and intangible, and within each group the dimensions are split into core and supplementary values. The core values are those that are generic to the group; they apply in principle to all baked beans products. If you decide to buy baked beans it is likely that these are the dimensions that will influence your decision.

The supplementary values are those that are brand specific. They can, of course, apply to several different brands, but are not generic to the product group. The choice of a brand is determined by the total strength of the various dimensions in relation to the perceived price. In a market that is heavily segmented the supplementary values have considerable strength; in a large, unsegmented market the core values dominate, and if one brand is dominating it has a strong identification with the main core values.

Tangible values

The tangible values are created by physical product features. That usually makes them easier to define and evaluate. For instance, if one can of baked beans has more beans than another, or if one pack of fish fingers is made from pure cod fillet and the other from minced fish flesh from an unidentified species, the comparisons are easy to make.

The more crowded marketplace and the intensified competition has, in many markets, brought about less product differentiation, which makes that type of comparison easier to do, but less relevant as the products are so similar. If all the products in a market sector offer the same perceived factual features, the comparison of tangible values obviously becomes less relevant. The definition of the dimensions are, though, still important as the analysis might divulge a way to make the one product really stand out, with a better perceived position than the others.

These 'hard' product values, the tangible values, form the basis for the appreciation of a product. All other dimensions will suffer if the tangible values are substandard.

Intangible values

The perceived value of a product is made up of not only tangible, but also intangible, benefits. While the tangible values are fairly easy to define and describe, the intangible values can be more difficult to deal with as they are by definition more subjective. Because of the very nature of an intangible value, such as 'traditional' or 'socially acceptable', any definition contains an element of subjectivity, while a tangible dimension is in principle based on an objective fact.

The general procedure for the evaluation of intangible values is the same as for tangible values. First, the important dimensions for creating the perceived values have to be defined. One needs to be fairly general at this stage to avoid having many more dimensions than are practically justified. In many markets, advertising has influenced the strength of intangible values. For instance, the relevance of the factor 'social acceptability' in the use of instant coffee is an effect of advertising. One has to recognize this and remember that the opportunity exists not only to create an advantage within one dimension, but also to improve the relative importance of a dimension in which the brand is rated favourably.

The intangible values are definitely most easily evaluated in a relative sense. It is easier to say that a Porsche is a sportier and more youthful car than a Rolls-Royce, than to put a figure on those values.

The difference between tangible and intangible values lies in how they are managed. That is the only reason for treating them separately. The management actions required to create and improve the two types of values are different, but the analysis and evaluations are similar. The intangible values are usually slightly more difficult to define, and the marketer probably finds it more difficult to be sufficiently objective when evaluating these values.

What one has to bear in mind in this situation is that any evaluation is better than none! Most marketing people with some experience can do most of the evaluation from their current knowledge. It is not necessary to be 100 per cent accurate, as it is only the general direction, not a detailed analysis to the nth degree, that is to be established. It is better to be 70 per cent accurate and get the results quickly than to be 90 per cent accurate and wait half a year for the results. The environment is dynamic; an old analysis is of no use as the competitive situation and, perhaps, the values of the customers will have changed.

The purpose of the analysis is to define the foundations on which one can build a better house with better walls, roof, etc. If the marketer waits too long, the circumstances will have changed.

Price

At a casual glance, establishing the perceived price of a product might seem an easy task. The price is, after all, on the price list or on the label. But that price information is like the tip of the iceberg. One must look at the price in a wider sense, in relation to the other goods in the marketplace that compete for the same purse. Determining this relative situation can be quite a challenge as, of course, at the end of the day everything competes. The line has to be drawn somewhere so the real, true competitors have to be isolated. This usually includes the other companies and brands selling similar products and, perhaps, one or two products outside of the product category itself. The similar products are there to represent the direct competition, and those products that are outside the product category indicate the generic competition for the product field. If one does an evaluation that also covers the past development, a retail price index comparison can be used as a 'generic' comparison.

The price survey will establish the factual, objective situation. It will give the establishment of the value balance a good start. However, performing a survey of the competitors' prices is nothing new; what *is* new with value-added marketing is that you have to look at the perceived situation. So instead of looking at the absolute prices on the list or the label, the marketer must get an understanding of the *perceived price*. Although the customers might not know the exact price of a product, they do have a view, a perception, of the price. It might be a very simplistic view, such as the product in question is 'expensive' or 'cheap', without having a specific figure to back up the claim; or it might be fairly precise – most housewives, for example, know the price of a joint of beef.

To use an example from the retail trade, most people would regard Harrods as an expensive shop and Kwik-Save as a cheap one. But to get someone to quote the price of marmalade in the two shops might be a bit more difficult (disregarding the fact that it might be difficult to find a customer who frequents both shops!). Another example, Nescafé Gold Blend is fairly expensive and Tesco Own Label Instant Coffee is less so. The customers know, certainly within a 10–20 pence ratio, the retail selling price of a grocery item such as instant coffee that is purchased with reasonable frequency; but for products with a more infrequent purchasing pattern the perceived price span is likely to be much wider.

The reasoning has a more dynamic dimension in that most judgements regarding price levels are made instantly, often without the total competitive factual knowledge. It is such a judgement that, to a large extent, determines whether the customer will or will not buy. The perceived price is set against the perceived value, the balance is evaluated against other products and a purchasing decision is made. These decisions are not elaborate, they cannot be if you consider that during a normal weekly shopping trip about 50 positive purchasing decisions are made within one hour (and perhaps 100 decisions not to buy).

The customer's perceived price may or may not be a correct reflection of reality, but it is nevertheless a very important factor in the value balance. If you expect to enhance the value of the products through the use of the value-added marketing concept, the complexity of pricing and perceived prices must be fully understood.

I once had the pleasure of meeting one of the most successful chief executives in a very specific field, the sales and distribution of frozen foods to the catering trade in France. His company had on the price list approximately 500 items. The company's turnover was over £200 million with a large workforce. In addition to all the facts this man had to know in running his business, he also knew the selling prices of all his main items. Not only that, he also knew how these prices were perceived by his main customer groups. He was instantly ready to discuss the current prices of cold water shrimps versus hot water shrimps and how the restaurants were coping with the price volatility on these items.

The perceived price information is also important for the pricing strategy itself. It can give the marketer indications as to whether the real price should be increased or decreased to maximize the revenue, and to know whether or not there is room for a price increase to pay for a more expensive and better product.

Detailed pricing knowledge, real and perceived, is invaluable information for a value-added strategy. It can only be acquired through a constant quest for more information.

Evaluation

The evaluation of the importance of the various dimensions is a two-stage process, going from *core values* to *supplementary values*.

The first step is to create an impression of how the customers perceive the product group. The various dimensions are evaluated and ranked. One can rank within the tangible values only, or, more appropriately, evaluate all the core values together. The customer is unlikely to make any differentiation between the two types of values, so why should the analyst do it? In our fictitious example, the ranking is illustrated in Table 7.2. At this stage only the core

Table 7.2 Ranking of core values (fictitious example)

Variable	Group evaluation
Growth	+5%
Market share	n/a
Tangible	
Core values	
Taste	1
Convenience	2
Filling	5
Supplementary values	
Versatile	x
Healthy	x
Intangible	
Core values	
Popular	3
Traditional	4
Supplementary values	
Children's favourite	x
Exciting to eat	x
Perceived price	cheap around 30p per can

values are considered as they are the only ones that refer to the product category.

The second step is the evaluation of the dimensions that make up the value balance of each individual brand. The core values, and the supplementary ones where applicable, are all evaluated in the form of a ranking or some other measurement (such as a scale 1–5). Some supplementary values are appropriate to many brands; some only to one.

Table 7.3 shows how brands A and B were ranked in the baked beans market. To make the exercise more useful, I have included key comments explaining the ranking to give a better overview of the situation to enable a decision to be made on how to enhance the various dimensions.

The value balance for the two brands A and B is now defined. It is obvious that brand B, with a 'healthy' positioning, has a much weaker taste preference and is less identified with the product group. It benefits less from the generic qualities and that is made worse by the fact that the attempt to segment the market and create a niche has been made at the expense of overall taste preference, which is the most important dimension. Sales have suffered despite

Table 7.3 Ranking of brands in the baked beans market (fictitious example)

Variable	Group evaluation	Brand ranking with comments	
		Brand A	Brand B
Growth	+5%	+2%	±0%
Market share	n/a	25%	10%
Tangible			
Core values			
Taste	1	2 Acid/sweet balance	7 Beans soggy
Convenience	2	4 M/w cooking instructions	3 ⎧ Higher ranking due
			⎨ to overall lower
Filling	5	6	4 ⎩ perceived value
Supplementary values			
Versatile	x	7 Recipe suggestions featured on can	–
Healthy	x	8 As brand leader, generic effect	1 Product feature, low sugar, high fibre
Intangible			
Core values			
Popular	3	5 More specific image (Children)	2 Generic effect
Traditional	4	1 Brand heritage	5 Specific product claim has made B less traditional
Supplementary values			
Children's favourite	x	3 Long-term advertising effect	–
Exciting to eat	x	9 Not featured, some generic effect	6 Product claim and advertising effect
Perceived price	Cheap, around 30p/can	Price leader, inexpensive, about 5p more expensive than average	Average for sector, cheap in some outlets

a specific product claim, as the claim is of minor general importance. On the other hand, the health benefit has made it possible to have a profile, although advertising investment has most probably been lacking as the intangible values are relatively weak.

By adding a few significant market facts the evaluation is made more relevant. The growth rate for the total market is included as well as the rates for the two brands, and the respective market share is in effect an illustration of the result of the value balance.

The next step is the full competitive evaluation, as shown in Table 7.4, as a comparison of each dimension from the viewpoint of brand B. If the supplementary values are distinct for each brand, it might be helpful to take all the supplementary values for each brand and

Table 7.4 Full competitive evaluation of Baked Beans (fictitious example)

Variable	Group evaluation	Brand ranking with comments		Evaluation, brand B strengths and weaknesses
		Brand A	Brand B	
Growth	+5%	+2%	±0%	
Market share	n/a	25%	10%	
Tangible				
Core values				
Taste	1	2 Acid/sweet balance	7 Beans soggy	Weakness
Convenience	2	4 M/w cooking instructions	3 Higher ranking due to overall lower	Slight weakness
Filling	5	6	4 perceived value	Equal
Supplementary values				
Versatile	x	7 Recipe suggestions featured on can	–	Weakness
Healthy	x	8 As brand leader, generic effect	1 Product feature, low sugar, high fibre	Strength
Intangible				
Core values				
Popular	3	5 More specific image (Children)	2 Generic effect	Weakness
Traditional	4	1 Brand heritage	5 Specific product claim has made B less traditional	Weakness
Supplementary values				
Children's favourite	x	3 Long-term advertising effect	–	Weakness
Exciting to eat	x	9 Not featured, some generic effect	6 Product claim and advertising effect	Strength
Perceived price	Cheap, around 30p/can	Price leader, inexpensive, about 5p more expensive than average	Average for sector, cheap in some outlets	

judge them on an aggregate basis, evaluating first all tangible values and then all intangible values.

The illustrated evaluation is made from a purely relative standpoint. It is the strength of brand B versus brand A that is considered, and the objective in this example is to create a basis for improving the relative position of brand B.

From the value balance one can also draw other conclusions, which can provide additional insights into the product category. For instance, the general value balance for brand A is superior to brand B. A high percentage of consumers are prepared to pay significantly more for brand A than the average for the category. It is in a true benchmark brand situation because of the heritage and the way the product has become the category standard regarding taste.

Brand B is weaker, it sells for two reasons, perhaps with little cumulative effect across the two dimensions. Some buy the brand because of the health claim; others buy it because it is cheaper, while maintaining a general positive generic standing. Any potential strengthening of the specific values (healthy and exciting to eat) have to be made with some care if the company wishes to avoid alienating some of the existing customers.

For brand B it might also be worth while doing a more detailed price evaluation. As the product is selling at different pricing points in different shops, it may be possible to increase (or perhaps decrease) the price to achieve higher overall profits.

Conclusion

The application of the concept of establishing the value balance will bring a much greater distinction to the marketing decisions. Each decision can be measured against the effect it will have on the balance; each competitor's strong and weak points will be defined; and the establishment of the balance will require of the marketer a thorough analysis of the real issues behind a product's performance.

The establishment of the value balance will make value-added marketing possible.

8

The role of market research

For marketing in the 1990s, and in particular when applying value-added marketing, it will be even more essential than ever to have a very thorough knowledge of the marketplace. In a competitive struggle, information about potential customers as well as rivals can be of crucial importance. There are many ways in which one can achieve such knowledge. The classical one is to commission market research.

Market research in this respect covers all the activities that a marketing department commissions to an independent agency, internal or external, in order to find out more about the customers and the markets. Market research is not to be confused with the indispensable activity of accumulating as much information as possible about a specific market and its customers and competitors. Market research is only one of several methods to build that bank of knowledge.

Is market research an efficient way of building knowledge? One way of determining whether a type of marketing activity is useful or not is to look at the correlation between the amount of money spent on that type of activity and the commercial success rate within specific companies. For instance, there exist several studies of the correlation between advertising expenditure, brand share and profitability. I have found no such study on market research. This should not come as a surprise as a high investment in market research is usually the sign of a company with an indecisive management that does not know its customers and does not have the thorough knowledge to allow it to make the right decisions immediately. Such a company does not only rely on market research, it is also unlikely to be profitable.

The weaknesses

While in theory market research is a useful activity as it generates information about the customers and the market, it usually falls short of this for three reasons: it is slow, it reflects history and it is subjective under the pretence (mostly of the marketers and not the institutes) of being objective.

The reliance on market research is one reason for classical marketing's overall slow approach to business, as discussed earlier. In the author's view, there are no objective reasons why market research should be slow. It is the way it is integrated and used in the classical marketing approach that makes it slow. From the briefing of a research project to the supply of the data, in theory, the time span does not need to be more than 1–2 weeks with modern computer technology. In reality it is 1–2 months, and while the project in question is in research, nothing happens because everyone is awaiting the report and the results.

Market research is conservative, it reflects yesterday's world. All market research analyses are based on 'yesterday's' facts and views. The data, whether they are quantitative or qualitative, are based on what has happened in the past.

Many research reports feature customers' projections of future development. While this might be of use in a business-to-business environment, for the FMCG market it is only a reflection of the mood on the day of the researcher's visit or telephone call.

The view expressed might still be valid, at least if it is evaluated with the full knowledge of the parameters of the consumers' actual situation, but it has to be judged with caution.

A significant factor in this context is the time span from the day of the research to the day of implementation. If you ask consumers whether they would like to buy the products they have been shown in a test situation, their answers are most probably a valid reflection of their views that day. It is also likely that if they are asked the same question a month later, they will answer in the same way. On the other hand, with the length of time involved in product development, the actions taken on the basis of the research might not be relevant until a year later, by which time the consumers will have modified their attitudes.

As explained in Chapter 4, the very successful Japanese consumer electronics companies have a totally different attitude. They test in real life with instant feedback, and use the knowledge not only to modify the products that are tested but to develop the vision of the ultimate product so that product development can continue beyond what market research can evaluate.

Market research is subjective, more or less. Much time and money is spent on trying to understand the customers through attitudinal data and other qualitative studies with often dubious results. In certain situations those kind of studies can play a role when the 'map' of the competitive landscape needs to be clarified. The usefulness of qualitative studies depends on interpretation and analysis. As the customers (who supply the information) and researchers (who analyse the information) are only human, the results of most attitude studies are at best imprecise, influenced by the personal views of the individuals involved.

How to acquire market information

What is much less subjective than qualitative studies, and in many instances give very objective data (and data that should be studied with great care), are studies that relate to the real actions (usually purchases) of the customers. A purchase is real; it is something that is done to achieve a specific objective; it is something that is done in the light of a certain perceived value for money. Data describing purchasing activities looked at in a critical and creative way can often tell a much better story than sophisticated and expensive attitudinal studies.

The marketing staff has to be in touch with, and understand, what is happening in the marketplace to be able to make the correct decisions. The best way to achieve that is for the marketer to *personally* stay in contact with the customers, talk to them and/or take all opportunities to be a customer. Although any personal dialogue with a customer is bound to be biased and unrepresentative, the quality of the information is better. It is better because it is direct, has no filters in the shape of interviewers or analysts, and the marketer can personally see the context in which a comment is made. With experience of first-hand contacts, the marketer will develop the skills to evaluate direct consumer dialogues. A conversation with a customer can be a most enlightening experience. It is no coincidence that the two leading supermarket chains in the UK, J Sainsbury's and Tesco, both have chief executives who take great pride in making frequent visits to their shops to meet customers (and staff).

This type of first-hand qualitative information has to be complemented with other sources as time and other practicalities restrict the possibilities to pursue the personal approach to its full potential. The role of market research is to complement the personal experiences; the personal experiences should not be complementary to the market research.

The consumer dialogue and the evaluation of sales data will generate information on the market. To evaluate products the best test is to be a consumer. If the marketer buys and uses the products, then first-hand knowledge of a superior quality will be obtained. Frequent usage of the marketer's own products and those from the competitors is essential to build up experience and is the best way of acquiring an understanding of why products are bought.

Formal market research can offer a lot of additional information, but this information must be carefully evaluated in order to avoid getting the wrong impressions or even making incorrect decisions. Just as cigarette packs carry a health warning, qualitative market research should similarly carry a warning saying that excessive use and extensive analysis can be dangerous to the health of the business. An over-reliance on market research means that management is out of touch with the actual customers and that they have abdicated part of their decision-making responsibility to the interpretation of market research. It is an altruism that the customer is the ultimate judge, but this is asking 'normal' people in a market research situation to 'make decisions' that management do not want to make.

The following example, from the launch preparations of the Lean Cuisine frozen prepared meals, shows how the conservative nature of market research can make otherwise very skilled people recommend the wrong action.

EXAMPLE In 1981, Nestlé's Stouffer's in the US launched Lean Cuisine, a range of superior quality prepared meals with a calorie content of less than 300 per serving. From Day 1 the range was a fantastic success; the trade called it 'The biggest thing in frozen foods, since frozen foods'.

To investigate the concept's viability in the UK for Findus, the Nestlé frozen food subsidiary, a very ambitious study was made by the research department of a big New York advertising agency, in cooperation with their London office. The compilation of data and the analysis were most impressive. All kinds of socio-economic facts and ratings of attitudinal statements were compared and investigated (it has to be added, no real product was shown to the customers). The final outcome and recommendation of the advertising agency was that there probably was a chance of success for Lean Cuisine in the UK, but it would in no way be as great as in the US.

According to the report, the UK consumers were not at the time ready for the Lean Cuisine concept as they were only moderately interested in 'fitness' and 'quality' (compared to the US) and the market position of premium frozen foods was weak. The results were a true reflection of the situation at the time

(1983) but the attitudes were about to change and the reason the UK consumer had only limited interest in premium frozen foods was that, up to that time, no one had marketed superior quality frozen foods (not to mention that the late 1970s and early 1980s were not a time for luxury goods compared to mid and late 1980s). Fortunately Findus did not take the advice to wait for the 'right' moment. They launched Lean Cuisine in January 1985 because the view of the management was that at the launch date the timing would be right. This turned out to be the correct conclusion. The range was launched and became the UK frozen food success of the decade, because in 1985 the consumers were interested in health and fitness. By then they were also prepared to pay a premium for an excellent quality product. Society changed from the time of the compilation of the research data to the moment of launch. The consumers started to buy premium products when they realized the type of quality they could get. Reality had proved research wrong.

On the other hand, in the preparation for the Lean Cuisine launch, research was used to confirm the product range and to develop the communication. Once the strategic decision was made, it was essential to expand the knowledge of the marketing department in this particular product area and to get ammunition to convince the retail trade to list the range. Product research (testing recipe preferences) and communication research (testing the appeal of advertising) were put to good use and provided valuable information. In that way research was used to enhance the (potential) customer knowledge, but not to make strategic decisions.

Market research does have a role to play. It can, if correctly planned and utilized, complement and expand the knowledge that, ideally, should already exist in the company. It is very important that the marketing management is totally aware of the customers and their views. This, however, is difficult, or even impossible, to achieve in the FMCG business without first having research programmes. It is difficult because there are too many customers and not enough time.

Management must not abdicate the business leadership to the market research department and the research consultants' interpretations of the views of the customers. An entrepreneur takes the decisions personally and bases those decisions on acquired knowledge.

Conclusion

The role of market research is to complement the business knowledge. Market research should have the role of helping the marketing people to define the product 'map', but which route to choose is a decision that has to be taken by managers.

Value-added marketing is about improving the perceived value of products and services. Market research has to be looked at in the same way. The marketing departments that buy the information and the companies that sell the data need to be aware of this. They should constantly strive towards achieving a value-for-money balance that will make their products, the studies, better value for their industry.

Market research has a place but the marketers must not over-estimate the ability of the discipline. It can give marketers information about their customers that would be impossible to acquire any other way. The hard quantitative data are, with very few exceptions, to be preferred over the soft qualitative information, as the former is closer to a real purchasing situation.

All research data are based on the past and can only be used to explain the situation as it was, not to predict what it will be. It can outline the map, but it cannot advise on the route.

9

Implementing value-added marketing

The main objective of the marketing department is to maximize the relative perceived value of the products for which it is responsible. The process of achieving an improved value balance involves many different types of activities and executional methods. Although it is inadvisable to be too systematic, a methodical approach will avoid confusion and waste of resources.

Most products contain a full spectrum of different types of values and there are even more ways of improving them. The marketer must develop a view of how the values of the products are to be enhanced, in a one- or multi-dimensional way, by focusing on building the attraction or the over-satisfaction, and how the short and the long term are to be balanced.

Vision

Every marketing executive knows about the importance of having clear objectives. It is a management axiom that an effective operation or project requires well-defined targets. Similarly, for the value-adding process the objectives must be clearly defined. I am not in this context referring to the overall purpose of value-added marketing, but to the desired end-result of improving a product. The executives must have a well-developed view of what the ultimate product should represent and what qualities it should have. To have a *vision* of the ultimate product is extremely important. The vision is the target, and the objective is that the building of values should come as close as possible to the vision.

The vision cannot be a competitive product, because if it were, the development target would be to create a 'me-too' product. Instead the vision is the marketer's dream of how to please customers. A quote from Mary Fox Linton, London interior decorators, 'Never

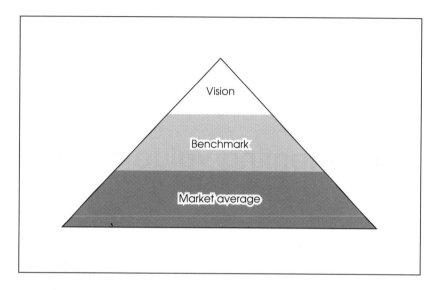

Figure 9.1 The concept of vision

give clients what they want, give them what they never dreamed they could have', is an excellent explanation as to how a product vision should be formulated. The vision has to go beyond the realm of the customers' current thoughts while, on the other hand, if the vision was to be explained to the potential customers each would say, 'Fantastic, just what I want'.

Each market segment has a benchmark, usually the brand leader or a company with a very strong quality perception. Heinz Baked Beans, Birds Eye's Fish Fingers, Nescafé, and Marks & Spencer's chilled ready meals are all benchmark products or brands in the UK. If a company has a benchmark product it is obviously not enough to stay on that level; and if others only match the benchmark product, then that is not adding enough value, it is just creating a me-too. To know where to move, beyond the benchmark, there must be a vision of a better can of beans, fish finger, cup of coffee or chicken curry (Figure 9.1).

Just as a product's value is multi-dimensional, the vision of a product must be created around a number of dimensions, both tangible and intangible. It is a dynamic process. The vision of today is not the same as next year's vision because over the year the market will have moved forward. The development of the vision over time is a gradual process; one dimension might stay the same for many years, while others change every year. It all depends on the circumstances, such as the technical and commercial progress.

Long term/short term

There are, in all companies, activities that are very short term (such as sale promotions) and some that are long term (for instance, development of new concepts). The conflict between the short term and the long term is classical and will probably never end. There is relevance to both perspectives. Just as it is true that with no short-term success there will be no long term to worry about, it is equally true to state that for a business to survive in the longer term, there has to be long-term activities. The lead time for technical developments in the product category to be converted into actual product changes is often the determining factor of how the long/short-term mix should be handled. If a product range is produced on equipment that takes two years to build, one must carefully consider the longer term. On the other hand, if 'everything' can be done in two months, only the vision needs to be long term, not the work. In most cases one will get the best long-term commercial results by balancing the type of activities that will give results in the short term – usually projects that are realistic and generally down to earth – and those that will take a long time to give a return. These are often of a speculative nature and slightly out of the ordinary.

A balance between the long-term and the essential short-term development of product features makes a good mixture. Sales will receive a boost in the short term while, at the same time, preparations are made for the long-term development.

Single- or multi-dimensional attack

Regardless of whether the emphasis is on long-term or short-term activities, one has to form an opinion as to how many issues a company and its marketing department can, or should, tackle at any one time.

Theoretically, for the process of adding benefits, a company can choose between a one-dimensional or a multi-dimensional approach. Obviously with a one-dimensional approach the marketer focuses all his or her efforts on improving only *one* dimension of the value balance. Take the example of a company making typewriters. A one-dimensional approach may mean that only the reliability of the machines is considered, with all the other possibilities for value enhancement, such as portability, speed and keyboard design, being ignored.

On the other hand, in the case of an extreme multi-dimensional approach, the marketer takes all imaginable dimensions and tries to improve them all in order to get the total perceived value to a higher level. In this situation, in the example of typewriters, it is not only the reliability that is tackled but also all the other dimensions, such as typeface, service, flexibility, portability, speed and design.

A one-dimensional approach is unlikely to be successful as very few products are bought and used on the basis of one single variable. In the multi-dimensional approach, the range of variables can easily become too wide. Each of the tangible dimensions will not receive sufficient attention by the organization to be made demonstratively better and the end result becomes one of suboptimizing the total effort. In addition, too much change will be confusing for the customers. They will no longer recognize 'their' product. For the intangible values, too many variables will make communication incomprehensible for the potential customers. The customers will be bombarded with all kinds of messages and the consistency and credibility of the communication will suffer. A situation with a multitude of messages will also be too difficult for the brand manager to manage, and dividing the marketing resources will dilute the effectiveness.

Common sense, as always, must prevail. A strictly one-dimensional approach is seldom an appropriate route as this means that opportunities will be missed. Good ideas to improve the value will not be utilized and the consumers might leave the brand's products out of communicative boredom.

The alternative, that the marketer should tackle the full portfolio – that is, a true multi-dimensional approach – is also unlikely to be a wise choice. As described in Chapter 8 on the value balance, there are seldom more than six or seven dimensions that are relevant for the customers, it is definitely inadvisable to exceed that number. For improvement purposes it might even be sensible to choose only half of these (three or four) and then perhaps complement the issue with one or two that as yet do not form a significant part of the product's perceived value spectrum to attempt to create a stronger general value balance in the longer term. If we return to the example of the typewriters, it could be that customers and manufacturers have so far totally ignored the design variable, because all existing machines look very similar. A creative (and fairly cheap) way of enhancing their value would be to give typewriters a truly modern, hi-tech design.

In the selection of variables for improvement, it is tempting to be over-ambitious – for example, in a more mature product group, where many values have been accumulated over time. It is, of course, always possible to add tangible dimensions but with more variables there is the risk that each will have less impact. A better alternative might be to abandon a few dimensions that have become old-fashioned and, in doing so, give the newer ones greater impact.

There are, of course, exceptions. If the variables are all within the same general sphere it is possible that the cumulative effect will be greater than the sum of the parts. In the 'healthy' baked beans example used earlier, it would for instance be to the advantage of the product if more 'healthy' dimensions were introduced, such as added vitamins or minerals. The combination of the new health claim with the old is likely to give the value balance a significant boost.

The risks involved in dealing with many dimensions are even more relevant in the case of intangible values. Too many values to communicate will make the total flow of messages unnecessarily confusing; a few clearly understood and relevant intangible dimensions make the communication more manageable for both the sender and the receiver. The message can well be multi-faceted and be the result of agglomerating several value dimensions, but the communication effect will suffer if it is fragmented.

The car industry provides us with a number of good examples of how to deal with this issue. A car is a complex piece of engineering. In the design of the car, many aspects are considered, such as comfort, speed, appearance, handling, etc. In the communication the successful ones focus on one dimension, even if the car has competitive advantages in other areas. Volvo focuses on safety, Audi on 'Vorsprung durch Technik', Saab on airplane heritage, and so on. For less complex products the alternatives are fewer so the choice should be easier. The success lies in the communication of only *one* value that makes the product initially 'attractive' as it generates interest in a single-minded way, but the reality of all the other variables (through product trial/usage or secondary communication) creates an attractive total product value.

There are, though, circumstances in which a totally one-dimensional attack is advisable. For instance, sometimes companies get into situations where the market position has seriously deteriorated because the management has allowed one crucial element in the perceived value set to slip. A total commitment to improving this one factor in order to get the company back on the right track may well be the best way forward. This one 'slipping' factor is usually product quality. In its eagerness to push for short-term profitability, the management have been tempted to cut down on the product quality. That has led to serious deterioration of, firstly, sales and, secondly, morale, so a strong programme to put the company back on stream will become a necessity. For such a company a single-minded quality improvement programme over 6–12 months will be the most viable route.

The number of variables to be dealt with over a specific time period should be related to the general situation of the product, as analysed in the value balance and the capacity of the organization. It is usually better to be conservative about how much you should deal with. If a value enhancement is to have any positive effect on customers it has to be sufficiently significant to be perceivable.

Building attraction or over-satisfaction

A further, important, choice to be made is between those activities that improve the attraction (the pre-purchase value) and those that improve the over-satisfaction (repeat purchase rate). The importance of achieving over-satisfaction has been explained earlier in the text; and a high repeat purchase rate is undoubtedly of fundamental importance to the success of any business. One cannot, however, disregard the attraction values. Even a well-established product needs to recruit new customers to expand its penetration and to replace lapsed buyers. Fortunately, in most instances the factors that have a positive influence on over-satisfaction also have some effect on the attraction values (and vice versa).

Despite this overflow a choice must be made, and in order to get the emphasis right one approach has to be given priority. The main factors influencing the outcome of such a decision are the length of time the product has been on the market, the awareness versus the penetration of the product (is there a potential?), the customer turnover rate, the competitive pressure and the type of product.

Over-satisfaction and attraction are both important and they do interact, but the ability to create over-satisfaction that will result in a high level of repeat purchases is, with few exceptions, the most important one for building a sound business.

The relaunch concept

The value enhancement activities will result in a more appealing product. While the product value-added process in itself is continuous, the improvements can either filter through to the customers on an equally continuous basis or be presented in a more forceful way through a relaunch. The latter approach is, of course, especially suitable if the attraction values are improved as, with a relaunch, more awareness is created.

Traditionally a marketer will be tempted to use any change for the better as an 'excuse' to relaunch a product range. A relaunch is a distinct activity; it shows that you are doing something that is contrary to the normal day-to-day, step-by-step value enhancement which, perhaps, is unlikely to be widely noticed in a company. In addition, the distributive trade and even the customers are often quite favourably inclined towards a relaunched product. One has to remember, however, that the changes should make the value perceivably better. If the changes are only cosmetic, the positive effect, if any, will be very short lived.

The main reason for the high frequency of relaunches is that they are often the only remaining alternative by which marketing executives can make their mark. If they do not get the opportunity to launch a new product, or if their products do not generate enough revenue to warrant a large advertising budget, a relaunch is the one remaining possibility.

The relaunch concept is not an approach that should be ignored. It does give the marketer the chance to get the added values recognized, internally and externally. To be successful and to be worth the investment of the marketing funds it has to be based on real changes.

Selecting the dimensions

The selection of which dimensions to improve or discontinue or leave unchanged is very important and difficult. The analysis of the various dimensions when the value balance is established will give guidance. Usually the strong dimensions have to be kept to provide a foundation for the future, while the weak ones have to be either improved or allowed to disappear.

The criteria for the selection should be the expectation of the maximum perceived value and the highest sales revenue at the lowest cost. The selection of which activity(ies) to focus on should be based on the estimated return (= positive value balance effect) for the company otherwise the resources of the company are not being optimized.

In our fictitious example of baked beans in Chapter 7, the potential for improvement is split up into short-term and long-term issues (Table 9.1). If the potential for enhancement exists, the action required is described very briefly.

Table 9.1 Short-term and long-term potential for improvement in baked beans

Variable	Group evaluation	Brand ranking with comments — Brand A	Brand B	Evaluation brand B strengths and weaknesses	Short term Potential for improvement	Potential action	Priority	Long term Potential for improvement	Potential action	Priority
Growth Market share	+5% n/a	+2% 25%	±0% 10%							
Tangible *Core values*										
Taste	1	2 Acid/sweet balance	7 Beans soggy	Weakness	Yes	Review sauce recipe Improve beans	1	Yes	Recipe constraints by healthy position to be overcome	1
Convenience	2	4 M/w cooking instructions	3 Higher ranking due to overall lower perceived value	Slight weakness	Yes	Introduce m/w cooking instructions	3	No		
Filling	5	6	4	Equal	No			Yes	Evaluate adding filling ingredient	
Supplementary values										
Versatile	x	7 Recipe suggestions featured on can	–	Weakness	Yes?	Expertise is lacking		Yes	Buy in expertise?	
Healthy	x	8 As brand leader generic effect	1 Product feature, low sugar, high fibre	Strength	No			Yes	Investigate possibilities for healthier product	3

Intangible								
Core values								
Popular	3	5 More specific image (Children)	2 Generic effect	Weakness	No		Yes	With media support the generic effect can be made brand specific	See below
Traditional	4	1 Brand heritage	5 Specific product claim has made B less traditional	Weakness	No		No	Possible to improve but not desirable	
Supplementary values								
Children's favourite	x	3 Long-term advertising effect	–	Weakness	No		No	Leave as A is much stronger	
Exciting to eat	x	9 Not featured, some generic effect	6 Product claim and advertising effect	Strength	Yes	2 Invest more in media	Yes	Develop claims and ideas to make product more exciting	2
Perceived price	cheap, around 30p/can	Price leader, inexpensive, about 5p more expensive than average	Average for sector, cheap in some outlets	–	No	Unlikely that product features will be stronger short term	Yes	Aim for diminishing price gap	

Following the definition of possible areas for improvement, the various dimensions are evaluated against the vision, a priority ranking is established based on a cost/benefit estimate. These estimates are made in relation to the priority the customers give to the different variables as well as the competitive situation and the ability of the organization to accomplish the planned value enhancement. In Table 9.1, both in the short and long terms, priority is given to the taste dimensions which is ranked number 1 in the overall ranking and brand B is clearly at a disadvantage in comparison with brand A. Priority number 2 is given to establish a stronger intangible value to balance the brand leader (brand A) as well as it is considered essential to get away from the fairly generic impression of the brand.

Brand B, in the example, is in a fairly weak position and the priority has been given to retaining current customers. The chosen tangible dimensions will particularly affect the current target groups, but the advertising's main objective is to create stronger over-satisfaction values. The attraction will not change much, with the exception of some advertising effect. The media communication reaches a wider audience and as such strengthens the attraction. For the longer term, the attraction effect is given more emphasis in order to build a larger potential customer universe. The tangible 'healthier' product can bring in new customers as can a more appealing advertising campaign.

The values attached to a product or a brand have to be taken care of. An example of mismanagement of the intangible values was the branding policy of what was once British Leyland, the car manufacturer. The frequent changes of brand from Morris, Austin, and Wolsley, etc., to the British Motor Corporation, to British Leyland, to BMCL, to Austin Rover, and to The Rover Group (a few names may have been lost in the sequence) is a striking example of how one can lose intangible values. With each change an amount of invested value and positive heritage disappeared. It is certainly an over-statement of the case to say that the brand changes led to the decline of the company, but the example shows that a neglect of the values of a brand name leads to losses of perceived value.

The value-added marketer should consider one more fact before committing the company's resources to a value-added programme. It might be that the best payback on the investment in money and labour required is to leave the perceived value balance as it is and focus attention and energy on internal efficiency issues. In the eyes of the customers, the perceived value of the product is perhaps already far superior to the competitors', but the company's total profitability is lagging behind because of inefficient production or administration. By first improving the profitability, the company can generate additional funds which then can be used to improve the balance further, but with better payback as the relative profit will be higher.

Conclusion

All the decisions regarding which dimensions to improve, how many at a time, and of what type, will lead to a programme of enhancing the perceived value. The end result might warrant a relaunch if the changes are sufficiently significant. If not, the constant flow of improvements will filter through to the customers over time. In both instances the task is to select the factors that will create the optimal result and then to start the activities. Provided that the 'motor' in the process (i.e. the brand management) has the necessary experience to guide the work and make the right decisions, the process will be one of great dynamism, and is likely to engage the whole company.

The rest of the book is dedicated to showing how and where one can apply value-added marketing. I have taken the common areas for the marketers' daily toil, and looked at each of them from the new perspective. As each type of marketing activity can improve both the attraction and the repeat purchase rate (and in order to be practical), I have chosen to look at the possibilities for improving the perceived value from the angle of the type of activity rather than from the result that might be obtained.

To make the presentation easier to follow, and in order to be consistent with the concepts of the book, I have divided up the activities into those that are likely to result in better tangible product values and those that mainly relate to the intangible values. As the value balance consists not only of value but also of cost for the customers, pricing strategy forms the final part of the review of the marketing mix.

10

Building tangible values

Superior quality/performance is the most fundamental part of the product mix to achieve over-satisfaction. Advertising can do wonders, as can beautiful packaging, but if the product quality is poor, the communication exercise becomes a non-starter. 'You can fool some of the people all of the time, and all of the people some of the time, but you cannot fool all of the people all of the time' (Lincoln). Virtually all product success stories are based on a solid product – everything from Levi's jeans, the VW Beetle and Sony video recorders, to Nescafé, Pampers and Persil detergents. All these products have had excellent advertising support, but the appeal is based on superior product quality.

It would appear that the quality improvement process is not taken seriously enough in western FMCG companies. Market and niche suitability has been given greater emphasis. Also, the concern many traditional FMCG managers have regarding exceeding certain pricing points has meant that the quality, which often costs money, has been allowed to deteriorate. Many industries and businesses, such as the American and European consumer electronics industry, have suffered great losses and even disappeared because they have under-estimated the importance of (improving) product quality.

In contrast, the very successful UK retailers Marks & Spencer, J Sainsbury's and Tesco have put much emphasis on product quality and, as a result, have strengthened their positions. It is unfortunately sometimes so that, in the food business, companies that are producing own label products for M&S or J Sainsbury's, as well as their own branded goods, have a higher quality standard for the own label.

The recognition of the importance of quality for the running of a successful business is not something particular to the 1990s. It is claimed that Jean-Baptiste Colbert, Louis XIV's famous finance minister, wrote in 1664 to the king: 'If our factories, through careful work, assure the quality of our products, it will be to the foreigners' interest to get supplies from us, and their money will flow into the kingdom.'

It is an essential part of the marketing strategy that a product has to live up to the expectations of the buyer. Even though each purchase is influenced by all the intangible values that are tied to virtually all companies and products, the most important dimension will always remain the actual product performance. The use of a product must deliver over-satisfaction.

It used to be said, jokingly among marketing executives, that it is not enough to make a better mouse-trap, you have to tell the world about it. This is true. What is equally true is that it is not a good idea to make a different, repositioned mouse-trap if that mouse-trap is not distinctly better than the existing one. Applying value-added marketing will make the mouse-trap brand manager ensure that his mouse-traps are the best and, if necessary, different traps will be supplied for different problems.

Mouse-traps or not, there is no question that the most important factor in achieving a high repeat purchase rate is the real product performance, 'product quality'. It was the general decline in the emphasis on product quality, and the realization of its importance, that first made me define the value-added marketing concept. It is also the lack of respect for the necessity of continuous product improvements that has led the two great classical marketing nations, USA and the UK, to lose market share to aggressive product-focused countries such as Japan and Germany. In their famous book *In Search of Excellence* Tom Peters and Robert Waterman observed that the consumer goods companies they had selected as 'excellent' were not low-cost producers in its traditional sense. They were successful with the consumers because they offered 'service, quality and reliability'. The same message was highlighted at many of the conferences that were held at the end of 1989, debating what the new decade would have in store. In one of them an analyst at Shearson Lehman Hutton said, 'This new emphasis on genuine product differentiation rather than superficial "branding" would have far reaching effects on marketing itself. . . . The next wave of change in consumer products will be fuelled by research and development.' These and earlier quotes and rationales all point in the same direction: the 'hardware', the product quality, must always be given first priority in a value enhancement programme.

Product quality

Product quality is a subjective value in that it is partly a personal
evaluation. Certain dimensions can be measured objectively, such as
how many times a tooth-brush can be used or the amount of a
certain ingredient, but many others such as the taste of a food
product is a subjective evaluation. Quality is made up of a multitude
of different variables. The methods of achieving a high quality, and
the dimensions that are most important, differ from product to
product, company to company, and even customer group to
customer group. The most important dimensions for a specific
product will have to be defined in the value balance analysis, and
are almost certainly clear to most people within an industry. Even
so, occasionally it might be worth while looking outside of the
traditional factors in order to avoid missing an opportunity to
enhance the quality in a more effective way.

Of course, one has to evaluate the quality in a relative sense. The
only relevant comparisons are those that the customers are making.
It is irrelevant to compare a Rolls-Royce to a Mini, but you can
compare a Jaguar with a Mercedes, or a Fiat with a Renault. On the
other hand, in certain situations the relevance covers a fairly wide
area. While there are perhaps few real alternatives when buying a
car, there are many alternatives when you want to buy a bag of
frozen peas. The quality of a specific brand of peas will not only
have to compare favourably with other brands of peas but also with
most other vegetables. (As a comment, the reason for the popularity
of frozen peas is that they 'freeze' much better than many other
vegetables. This is why the perceived relative quality of the frozen
green pea is traditionally so high.) If the relative quality of the peas
of a certain brand deteriorates, the customers might change to
another brand, but they might also change to a totally different type
of vegetable.

Quality improvement is a relative concept and in order to move the
product forward in quality terms one needs to look at all the
possibilities for improvement. Firstly, the product must be strong in
the basic, industry wide, quality dimensions, and, secondly, it can
be useful to look outside the obvious to gain a competitive
advantage. As an example, a basic quality requirement for a tape-
recorder is that the machine records and plays in a fully satisfactory
way; a secondary feature can be that it also has a direct radio
recording feature. In today's world that is an obvious quality issue; a
few years ago it was a luxurious added benefit. The electronics
companies have moved the goal posts and to compete successfully

you must be the company that moves the posts, rather than one that follows others.

Production quality

Quality improvement does not stop at the design board. It is as important, and in certain instances more important, to ensure that the production process consistently delivers the quality level that has been decided. It is not unusual that poor manufacturing standards – whether they are in traditional manufacturing or in the service industry – have let entire companies and even industries down. Also, it is not unusual to hear irate customers deciding never to use a brand again because of poor workmanship. Examples of this are unfortunately quite common, parts of the British car industry in the 1970s being a classical case.

A more positive example, in which the commitment to quality has really made a difference, is McDonald's. It is an unquestionable fact that part of the success of McDonald's, if not the main reason, is their total commitment to product quality. McDonald's hamburger is 'manufactured' on-site, the various components are delivered to the restaurants, the meat is cooked and the burger assembled. One can describe McDonald's as a totally decentralized manufacturing operation with a retail unit attached. To achieve a common standard across thousands of manufacturing sites was and is a tremendous task, not made easier by the fact that the units are not owned by McDonald's, but by franchisees. It is often forgotten that many hamburger chains have made better tasting hamburgers and were in the market long before McDonald's. The difference was that no one but McDonald's had the fortune to have a leader as committed to quality as Ray Kroc. His 'obsession' with quality, service and cleanliness (QSC) has meant that only McDonald's delivers such a totally consistent quality. The customers can be sure that the Big Mac they order is always of true McDonald quality, whether it is bought in Chicago, Florida, London, Geneva or Moscow.

The McDonald story holds a number of lessons, but we shall list only two: (1) to succeed you do not have to invent, you only have to know how to do 'it'; and (2) continuity and commitment in the execution are crucial.

The original McDonald brothers founded their first and only fast-food restaurant, a drive-in, in 1937 in California. They were very successful and soon had a very good business. Unfortunately, their success was not without problems and running a drive-in with a fairly extensive menu meant that there was a lot of waste in cutlery and raw materials. Consequently, the business was revamped and totally changed in 1948 to a hamburger-only restaurant with service windows. The menu was very limited and 'proper' cutlery was not used, only paper and plastic. The McDonald unit offered a standardized product, but excellent quality and fantastic value for money as it was selling hamburgers at half the price of what the competition charged (15 cents against 30 cents).

Sales were very satisfactory and so were the profits, the volume growth compensating for the lower prices. In order to maximize revenues from their site they developed what was to become the core of the McDonald manufacturing idea, the method to produce hamburgers in a super-efficient way. The brothers invented tools and procedures to achieve a quicker and more standardized method of preparation. The hamburger was not the invention, it was the methodology that was new. The tools and the (strictly enforced) methods guaranteed a consistent quality at a low cost. Anyone can make a hamburger, the McDonalds had invented a way of making it fantastic value for money: excellent quality, fast service and inexpensive.

The McDonalds were not interested in expanding beyond their own outlet. The man who did that was the legendary Ray Kroc, the founder of the modern McDonald's. He took over the licensing of the McDonalds' ideas in 1955.

While McDonald's have not deviated from the basic idea over the years since 1955, the menu and the execution are constantly revised and improved. The organization is today as committed to the QSC as it was in the 1950s, but the operation is constantly looking for improvements. Experiments within the framework is encouraged. Some initiatives succeed, such as the chicken nuggets; others fail. Regardless of the product or the country, the basics of the operation are still tightly controlled, the McDonald's operations manual is a classic in the food service trade and its enforcement is extremely detailed. The end result of applying to the humble hamburger an inventive and committed quality manufacturing philosophy is a world leader with an annual turnover of over $10 billion and a very solid profit level. The reliability of McDonald's and the excellent value for money has made the hamburger chain a world-wide family favourite.

The quality aspect can never be seen in isolation. It can be enhanced by the other elements of the marketing mix. The Ronald McDonald character helps to build a positive perception of McDonald's quality just as the emotional Levi's advertising helps to sell jeans. The marketer has to be aware of the fact that if the tangible product quality is not up to expectations, the efforts to build a strong perceived value will be in vain. A customer can be 'fooled' once or maybe twice by strong attraction values to buy a product, but if the product performance disappoints there will be no repeat purchases.

Renovation and reformulation

The most tangible value, the product quality, can be enhanced in different ways. The approach is not the same for a FMCG company as for a single product industrial company; nor is it the same for a retailer as for a car company. The common denominator is the ultimate result: a better product that is perceived by the customers as such.

When starting up a product improvement programme, the importance of having a vision becomes clear. To search for improvements without a goal would be very wasteful and frustrating. Virtually all successful business people have a vision of what they want to achieve. The vision of the ideal product must be well defined in the minds (and hearts) of all brand managers. The vision will provide a benchmark, and the product enhancement is a constant struggle to come as close as possible to that benchmark. Usually the most difficult part of the struggle is not to achieve the target/vision but to do so while also improving the perceived value balance – in other words, without letting the improvements cost too much.

The improvement in quality can take the shape of a renovation or a reformulation process. The renovation process covers everything from a minute change in a product – 64 per cent fish fillet instead of 63.5 per cent in a fish finger – to the biggest change one can make without altering the character of the product, such as changing the crumbs in the coating and the type of fish.

A product reformulation is more drastic. The entire character changes, such as when the fish finger was given a wholemeal coating. The product retained the basic characteristics of a fish finger but had a different flavour and a healthier image.

Each product that is being sold has some inherent value for customers, otherwise no one would buy it. It is important not to throw that value away, but rather to define it and improve on it. The amount of value that can be retained influences the choice between renovation or reformulation.

The decision is, of course, influenced by many other factors: what is the market like?; what do the customers appreciate?; how are the competitors' products perceived?; and so on. If the product is in a strong and healthy situation, a renovation programme is most likely to be the best route; if sales are slipping because of decreasing rates of repeat purchases, a more drastic reformulation project might be necessary. A further difference between the two alternatives is that while almost all products, regardless of category can benefit from a renovation programme, many products will not benefit from being reformulated. A reformulation can easily result in the decline of some valuable perceived dimensions as the product's character is changed. If so the end result of the whole process might not be beneficial for the company. That does not mean that the reformulation alternative can be ignored. It must be a priority awaiting opportunities to arise. A technological breaththrough can open up possibilities, or the consumers' expectations might change.

The vision and understanding of the expectations of the consumers are important factors in the decision on how to tackle the improvement of the quality dimension. The renovation process is constant and needs to be managed as such. The reformulation of a product is something that happens, perhaps, every 5–10 years. A comprehensive programme covering both options is essential for the longer term building of product values. In order to be worth introducing, the improved product values must always improve the perceived value balance, and to make commercial sense the company's input in costs have to be less than the income generated by the perceived improvement by the customers.

An example from a rather special sector of the consumer market is Lego, the Danish toy company founded in 1934, although the famous plastic building bricks were not launched until 1949. According to the *Financial Times*, Lego has world-wide sales in excess of $1 billion. The business strategy is said to centre on long-term product development, although product adaptation and utilization are better terms as the basic product, the building block, is always the same. The variants of the block and how to put them together in kits are constantly revised (developed). At any one time there are approximately 300 kits for sale, at a unit cost ranging from less than £1 to over £100. The kits comprise about 1300 different shapes, all based on the Lego block. The constant innovation and high quality sets Lego apart from its competitors in the toy industry. From the *Financial Times*: '"With Lego, you push out a lot of product at a steady pace", says Liz Tanner, a buyer at Hamleys, the large London toy shop.' About one-third of the range is renewed each year, giving each item a fairly short average life span (2–3 years). While other toy companies rapidly move from one niche concept to another searching for a new Barbie or Transformer, Lego has stuck to its knitting, but with constant improvements and a very strong emphasis on quality. '"We have demonstrated continuity, but with change", says Kristiansen, a quietly-spoken 42-year old who has headed Lego since 1978.' The constant adaptation of the basic product has meant that Lego has maintained a very strong market position despite other companies copying the block-idea and the disappearance over time of some basic patents.

The Lego philosophy is in stark contrast to that of a similar concept, Meccano. Once a popular British product it was just not adapted and improved, so it almost totally disappeared.

Reversed salami tactics

The process of increasing the perceived real product value is in effect a reversed value analysis. Value analysis was very popular during the 1960s and the 1970s. The application of value analysis led to the implementation of the 'salami' tactic that ruined many products by undermining the product quality. By slicing off 'bits' of the quality at each yearly product review, the products eventually deteriorated to such an extent that they were abandoned by the customers. Each slice was so thin that it was not noticed, but after a couple of years the product became a pale impression of its former self. The tactic to save money became a tactic to lose customers.

The objective of that type of value analysis was a reduction in the production costs, with the end result of a cheaper product in more senses than one. Value-added marketing represents the reverse, a much more positive approach of seeing how value can be *added* to improve the product quality. Just as the salami tactic meant that sales declined, the reverse of the tactic, properly applied, means that sales will increase.

In this process of product improvement, which must never stop, one has to go through all the relevant dimensions of the product and evaluate them. As opportunities for improvements arise they must be evaluated to see if a change will improve the perceived value. If it will, the next question to be asked is: 'Will the improvement pay for the change if additional costs are incurred?'

I prefer to sound a word of caution in being too rationale in these situations. To be competitive in the 1990s, product quality and product performance will play greater roles than they have in the past. The implication for management is that they must show courage in deciding when to improve the quality of the products – to wear the hat of the entrepreneur rather than the hat of the accountant.

Conclusion

A good understanding of the customers and the value dimensions of the product, and a well-defined view of what the ultimate product represents, are the key ingredients in a product improvement programme. Whether it takes the format of product renovation, reformulation, or higher manufacturing standards, the objective remains the same, a higher quality product giving the customer an enhanced value-for-money perception.

The product quality is the base on which the rest of the marketing programme is built. There is no sense in employing a good painter to make a house look beautiful with fresh colours if the walls are starting to crack and the roof is leaking. Similarly, it is not good business practice to spend a lot of money advertising a product if the quality is poor. On the other hand, a beautiful finish to a well-built house will add value beyond the cost. Thus, a well-executed advertising campaign for a high-standard product will be money well spent.

11

Old product development

The North American and European FMCG companies were the first to adapt the classical marketing principles of focusing the company resources on meeting customer needs and, by defining and exploiting unfulfilled market niches, building new business. Most, if not all, FMCG companies have continued to follow those principles despite diminishing returns on their efforts.

At the introduction of the marketing concept to a wider audience in the 1950s, the strategy of adapting a company's products to fulfil the consumers' needs and wants was a great step forward. But times have changed, and above all the competitive situation and the attitudes of the consumers in today's world bear little resemblance to the consumption-happy 1950s and early 1960s. The successful formula for prosperity of 20–30 years ago is now totally outdated, but the FMCG industry's marketing departments do not seem to have realized this. Enormous efforts are still put into researching and defining unfulfilled consumer needs, developing products to fit the needs, working out detailed marketing plans to pinpoint the exact positioning, and launching a great number of new products. All this despite the fact that the great majority of those new ventures will fail because those who 'need' form too small a percentage of the population or, more probably, because the new products will offer less appealing value for money as they are no better than those already available.

The established FMCG companies would be much more profitable if they were to redirect the new product development (NPD) efforts into taking care of their existing products and focus their attention on old product development (OPD).

Each company with significant sales in the consumer goods market has one or several valuable assets in existing products and brands. Every product that is sold has some sort of appeal, and rather than discard that value on the 'scrap heap' of discontinued products, it should be used as a foundation to make something better.

The definition

Old product development is the continuous process of improving
the perceived tangible value of existing products. It is the way to
add real product benefits to a company's current range of products.

If OPD is to be truly effective it must cover the totality of a product.
Not only must the 'old' product be developed but it is as important
to ensure that the existing or revised product is manufactured in the
most cost-effective way. Only through combining the improved
product quality with production efficiency can the perceived value
for money for the consumers, and thus company profitability, be
maximized.

Rationale

As explained earlier, several studies have been made on the (lack of)
success of new product introductions in FMCG markets. The studies
usually show that about 10 per cent of concepts that have been
initiated reach the marketplace and, of these, 25–30 per cent survive
the first two years. The statistics include all kinds of products, and
as the majority do not receive advertising support it is estimated that
each launch costs an average of £200 000. Of the approximately
12000 new food products launched in the US and western Europe
each year, at least 70 per cent are failures, at a cost of £1680 million.
If these resources were put to more efficient use, considerable
progress could be made.

This focus on NPD grew out of classical marketing's emphasis on
exploiting consumer needs. A new product is the logical answer to
an unfulfilled need. The main problem with this reasoning is that
people's product lives are, in most cases, already filled to the brim
so there are very few opportunities for new products. Because
resources have been channelled into new products, existing
products have been starved of innovation and product care and
have lost position to (in Europe) retailers' own label and small
producers.

The lack of new product successes described above is nicely
balanced by the previously quoted A C Nielsen study of leading
brands in the UK. The study was made in December 1989 and
showed that the average age of the top 10 brands in the consumer
market is 42 years. These top brands – Persil detergents, Nescafé
instant coffee, Whiskas cat food, Ariel detergents, Andrex toilet
paper, Coca Cola, PG Tips tea, Pedigree Chum dog food, Heinz

Baked Beans and Flora margarine – are the exceptions rather than the rule in the FMCG market. They have been managed with care over the years, been nurtured and the product carrying the brand has been subjected to reviews so that it has always offered the customer an attractive product.

The key to success with any grocery item is to offer the consumer superior perceived value for money. The well-established products have an instant advantage over any new product in value-for-money terms due to the way the retailers calculate their trade margins. On the 10 items listed in the previous paragraph the retailers take a lower margin than on equivalent new products. The difference is often 10 percentage points, sometimes more.

The retailers do this for several reasons. Firstly, a new product is a practical way of increasing the overall average margin, a long-term objective of most businesses. Secondly, a new product will, to a large extent, take sales from existing lines (cannibalization), so in expanding the range it makes short-term business sense to require a higher margin. Thirdly, new products and product proliferation cost the retailers (as well as the producer) money in administration and stockholding. Finally, a new product represents a risk, and, as many new products fail, the retailer likes to cover that risk through a higher margin. In contrast, an existing product is 'safe'; it sells through quickly making the turnover per linear foot high, thus achieving a reasonable total margin per shelf unit; and, perhaps above all, low prices on key household items is a way of projecting to the customers that a shop's price level is low. The consumers do not have detailed knowledge of individual prices, but a few key items are at the top of their list, and those create the price/value image of the store.

Considering that in the manufacturing trade profit levels are rarely over 5 per cent and the marginal contribution is 30–40 per cent on sales, a 10 percentage points difference in margin has a dramatic impact on (a) the profit for the supplier making room for marketing or production investments, or on (b) the RSP, improving the value-for-money perception for the consumers. Many FMCG companies are not in agreement with this mark-up philosophy by retailers, but it is a fact of life. It is foolish to ignore it, and it should be taken into account when planning the company's product portfolio. A new product's value for money will always be at a disadvantage to the existing big sellers by at least 10 per cent.

NPD programmes are wasteful and generally unsuccessful. New products are penalized, for good reasons, by the retail trade.

Meanwhile, old products can remain successful for decades if
properly managed.

OPD in relation to classical NPD

The main differences between OPD and classical marketing NPD are
listed below.

1 OPD starts with a vision that is created in the company; classical
   NPD starts with market research monitoring the consumers'
   wishes.

2 NPD aims to fulfil needs and wants; OPD improves something
   that is already 'acceptable' to achieve over-satisfaction.

3 OPD is a continuous process; NPD is intermittent and project based.

4 OPD means a stronger core business; NPD means a fragmented,
   or segmented, business.

5 OPD makes sales of best selling products even larger (with
   economies of scale in production and advertising); NPD splits the
   sales into many small products.

The OPD process

The objective with value-added marketing is to create the most
appealing product. Old product development is the method to
achieve that through existing products. The process is similar to
other aspects of value-added marketing: define a vision, then
improve the variables that will realize the vision.

OPD is not a singular project, such as the development of a new
product; it is rather a series of mini-projects, each resulting in a
minimal or significant change for the better. However, from a work
point of view it is exactly like NPD, setting an objective and
developing towards that target. An advantage with OPD is that the
subject for the project is a real product – it is 'alive', it is already
being used. That gives opportunities for the marketer to interact
with consumers and to have a dialogue with people who have
experience of dealing with the product, such as purchasing
managers regarding raw materials, production managers regarding
processing and sales managers regarding customer feedback.

Judging from the successful brands that follow the OPD principles,
one can draw the additional conclusion that changes affecting the

product should not be too frequent. These products are regularly used in the household and have managed to create a distinct profile. If many subsequent changes are made, the consumers acquire a feeling of uncertainty, and that can be almost as dangerous as not changing at all. People like familiarity, and need to become accustomed to one set of changes before they are confronted by the next.

The OPD programme will make the core products of a company stronger. It will create greater appeal for items that are certainly already on the shopping list, but with the OPD programme they will appear on more shopping lists or, more defensively, the OPD will ensure that they stay on the lists despite new competitors.

A higher sales rate of the core product means improved economies of scale. FMCG companies often neglect this very important point; they consider that market segmentation (fragmentation) will make them stronger with the consumer, neglecting the fact that it jeopardizes production and supply chain economics. To make money when competing with smaller manufacturers, who often have a lower overall cost base, an FMCG company needs to have the benefits of scale production. With the additional help of lower retailer margins the FMCG company arrives at a much more attractive economical situation than a company with a segmented product portfolio, where each new product is hit by top retail margins and short production runs. I shall later refer the example of Nescafé, but the company that has most successfully followed this principle in the UK is probably Heinz, with a strong emphasis on core products, heavy investment in production technology, reliable product quality and excellent financial results (a return on capital in excess of 20 per cent over several years).

The end result of a well-executed OPD effort is bigger profits from the core items. Those profits can be used to increase the dividends, but a more prudent approach is to invest in making the products even more attractive. Fixed investments in marketing support become less costly if the product has reached a higher sales level. Longer production runs can make investments in new technology more feasible, thus ensuring even stronger profitability in the future. Finally, the resources can be used for further work on OPD.

This positive cycle of investments and benefits can go on indefinitely (Figure 11.1). There is no reason for a product to decline unless the whole base for its existence disappears. 'The product life cycle theory is just a good excuse for bad marketing' is a very relevant statement. The OPD process has to be continuous. If it is stopped,

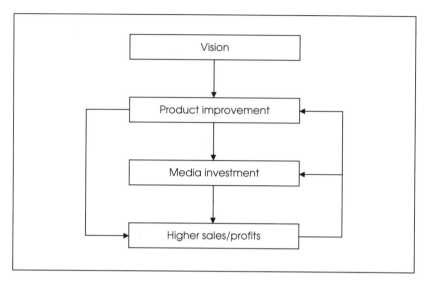

Figure 11.1 The positive OPD cycle

the products will lose their position sooner or later, and sales will start to decline.

The one thing that needs to be reviewed at intervals is the vision. Technology changes, habits change, consumers change, competition changes. All these factors make an occasional review of the vision necessary. Please note the term 'occasional'; if the review is too frequent it is no longer a vision but simply a series of day dreams.

OPD is not the same as the current fashionable term of leveraging brand strengths across product groups. OPD is about enhancing the real values of a product – making it better. Extending the use of a brand name (leveraging) is only a communication method of telling the consumers that a new (or old and renamed) product is made by the same people as an existing product(s).

Nescafé – an example of OPD

The development of Nescafé over the last 15 years is a fascinating story of how a brand has moved from a position of being a market leader, but vulnerable and constantly under threat from the competitors, to being an unassailable market dominant and one of the leading grocery brands. Even the Monopolies and Mergers Commission has acknowledged Nestlé UK's ability, stating in March 1991 that 'Nestlé's . . . profitability reflects its success in meeting consumer preferences in a market characterized by effective competition and a wide degree of consumer choice'.

Instant coffee is not a new product, nor is Nescafé a new brand. Nescafé – and, with it, instant coffee – was invented by the Nestlé Company in the mid 1930s in Switzerland (at the request of the Brazilian government) and launched in the UK in 1939. It has grown to become a household staple; today 93 per cent of all UK households use instant coffee.

The instant coffee market in the UK is huge, worth over £500 million at RSP. It is a virtually static market in volume terms.

While Nestlé UK as a totality is a profitable operation, in 1989 the return was 14.5 per cent on sales and 49 per cent on assets, it was not always so. From 1976 to 1980 the average return on investment on Nestlé instant coffees was at the fairly normal rate of 15.7 per cent, but by the end of the 1980s it had grown and the average for the period 1985–89 was 89 per cent.

The Nescafé product portfolio consists of 10 different products. The two core items, standard Nescafé and Gold Blend (a freeze-dried premium product), account for 84 per cent of total turnover. Several products cater for more specific tastes, such as the milder Fine Blend and the super premium Alta Rica blend, and Nestlé also has three decaffeinated variants. The role of the fringe products is two-fold: (1) to keep 'all' segments covered to avoid a potential competitor growing a strong niche presence, and (2) to make it possible to monitor at first hand any emerging trends. Nescafé is even present in the Roast & Ground sector (less than 10 per cent of the total coffee market) for these very reasons, although profitability is poor and volumes are low.

The instant coffee market is neither a homogeneous market nor one with little activity. There are over 200 different coffees being sold in the UK and an average supermarket stocks around 35 different packs of instant coffee. The Nescafé brands' total share of the market is 58 per cent in value, and 54 per cent in volume. The share has increased by more than 10 percentage points over the last 10 years, mainly at the expense of cheaper 'own label', despite frequent assaults by the main competitors, Kraft General Foods (Maxwell House) and Brooke Bond (part of Unilever). This is contrary to most other large FMCG brands in the UK who have lost share to 'own label' over the same period.

By the end of the 1970s Nescafé was a fairly lack-lustre brand, suffering from the price shock of 1976–77 when the raw material, green coffee beans, exploded in price from £1000 to £4000 per tonne. Competition was intense not only from other pure instant coffees but also from different types of cheaper coffee mixtures. The market was pushed down in quality terms as some manufacturers off-set consumer reactions to higher prices by cheapening the blends. The options open to Nestlé were either to take on competition on a short-term basis and fight with the price/promotional weapon or to take a long-term view and start to build a stronger quality lead over the opposition. The latter alternative was chosen.

The quality of a coffee depends on a combination of a number of different variables, of which the flavour dominates. The flavour is the result of the type of coffee beans that are used and the extraction/drying process. With Nescafé, the selection of the coffee beans was improved in two different ways. In the first, the blend of beans was changed. The amounts of cheaper qualities (Robustas) were decreased and the more expensive Arabica types were increased. This was a costly exercise, but was alleviated by the fall in raw material prices in the early 1980s. The second exercise was more long term. The selection of coffee beans was refined, with more detailed specifications for the qualities of the beans. Rather than just buying a specific type of bean (such as Robusta), an improved raw material examination procedure was installed. Each delivery was put through a much more rigorous evaluation of the various dimensions that make up the profile of a coffee. The evaluation obviously formed the base for the approval or rejection of the beans, but it also provided an instrument for a better definition of each delivery to enable it to be used for mixing the blend in the best possible way. The procedure resulted in a superior tasting coffee, but the effects will continue to appear as constant monitoring creates an ever-improving bank of expertise.

With richer and more expensive raw materials it became more essential to improve the manufacturing process. The Nestlé Company does not divulge its production technology, but substantial investments were made to retain more of the delicate coffee flavours in the final product. The manufacturing technology is a result of constant innovation from the central Nestlé research centres in Switzerland, coupled with local manufacturing know-how. New ways of processing are brought on stream with some regularity. Nestlé even extracts and saves the coffee aroma. With a patented process Nestlé ensures that each jar not only tastes well, but also gives that attractive coffee aroma.

The production process significantly influences the product characteristics such as flavour, solubility and aroma. These, together with the price of the raw material, are the main variables that determine the manufacturing cost of the product as the higher the process yield of the coffee beans, the more profitable a company will be.

Although it is fairly easy to gain access to instant coffee production technology, Nestlé has by now accumulated so much knowledge in the production of instant coffee that their superior quality is very difficult to replicate.

The product improvement programme behind Nescafé is the main reason why they constantly outscore competition in stores and in samplings. In blind tastings both Nescafé and Gold Blend receive preferential ratings of 10–20 per cent over the main competitors (with branded samples, the difference is much higher). This explains why Nescafé can maintain such a high brand share despite a premium price of around 5 per cent more than the number 2 brand and up to 100 per cent more than some cheaper brands.

It is fair to state that product quality is only one of the reasons for Nestlé's success. The enhanced quality, and the improved sales and profitability that followed, made it possible for Nestlé to spend more money on advertising to promote the brand. It is equally fair to state that the advertising is also of a very high standard.

With more communication, higher trial and repeat purchase rates have been achieved, resulting in more loyal users as the Nescafé quality is superior. More users generate more revenue, and with the extra revenue further investment can be made to improve the quality and promote the brand. Nescafé is now in a positive OPD cycle.

The reason for the redevelopment of the Nescafé products in the 1970s was not because the product was considered to be of poor quality or because market research showed that there was a need to improve the coffee. The consumers in 1975 were satisfied with Nescafé, which was, after all, the brand leader. The improvement programme was initiated because, firstly, it was in the Nestlé tradition to try to make the best coffee at an affordable price to ensure the long-term prospects of the business. Secondly, it was also the belief of the management at the time that future drinking habits (e.g. less milk and sugar in the coffee) would make the consumer more likely to appreciate a better quality coffee. The Nestlé management had a vision and sufficient confidence in their product and technology to embark on an expensive product improvement programme rather than stop, be content with a relatively good position, and fight the competition from that platform.

The combination of high-quality advertising and a superior tasting soluble coffee has made Nestlé UK one of the most profitable food and drinks companies in Great Britain and one of the Nestlé group's most profitable subsidiaries. But it took over 10 years!

Conclusion

Changing focus from NPD to OPD will affect a company's profitability in a positive way, but it will also influence the way in which the marketing department is being run.

The skills to run an OPD programme are very different from those required for a NPD programme. For NPD you need creativity to spot the opportunities, knowledge of other products to see parallels, enthusiasm to sell new ideas and to visualize new concepts. Experience and detailed knowledge of the market is less important as it can hinder a creative look at the product field.

For OPD it is important to understand the full product background and the values the consumers see in a product so that the base can be defined and the right variables can be chosen for improvement. It is important to understand how a product is made before you can suggest how it can be improved; you must also understand the customers so that changes to the product will be perceived as positive, not negative. On the other hand, it is less important to be very creative as the main dimensions are fairly well established through history. It is generally not a question of dramatic innovation, it is a question of modification – evolution, not revolution.

The grasshopping marketing executive of today, going from one job to another, making his or her mark in NPD through a creative application of imagination, is not the ideal candidate for OPD. OPD requires a thorough knowledge of the product and the market, and that only comes with time and experience.

Old product development is a neglected area among today's FMCG companies. Insufficient time and emphasis are given to the need to constantly update and improve existing products. Society is conservative and prefers familiarity, but the consumers, at the same time, will always appreciate a better product. In addition, the fact that the retailers' margin aspirations are different for existing and new products make OPD an even better proposition for the FMCG marketer.

12

New product development

New product development (NPD) has been one of the pillars on which many marketers have depended in their quest for success. By the very nature of the classical marketing theory – i.e. to aim for, to define and to exploit new segments of the market – NPD has been given much emphasis. A new product is the 'obvious' answer to an 'unfulfilled need'. It is also true to say that many companies have been quite successful in following the NPD route. By constantly launching new products they have managed to stay ahead of the competition. There are also many companies who, over the years, have wasted huge amounts on unsuccessful new product development programmes.

As markets change, opportunities for new products appear. The companies with a good NPD track record have had the ability to spot the right trends and develop products that have given the customers a better perceived value. For the future, the main problem is that the different FMCG markets are in general becoming more crowded, therefore there are fewer possibilities of launching successful new products that will reach high sales levels. In addition, the launch of a new product is also becoming more expensive in marketing costs. Product reformulation and renovation, where one is utilizing the investments that have already been made in perceived positive product values, is not only a more economical option but is also a generally more attractive alternative, as explained previously.

New products in the sense of this chapter are not launches of range extensions and similar modifications on a theme. Conceptually they are a part of the OPD programme for that range.

NPD in a classical sense

A classically trained marketer sees NPD as a key instrument in achieving the objective of fulfilling consumer needs.

In classical marketing the first step in an NPD process is to commission market research to find out what the customers think in an attempt to discover if there are any unfulfilled needs. With the help of the research the marketer tries to isolate unexploited segments in the marketplace. From an analysis of the available data, the market is reviewed and the new product opportunity is described in a market analysis. A brief is written and approved for the new product, which is then developed and launched. The time span of this process can be anything between 12 and 30 months. The consumer attitudes on which the NPD personnel are basing their launch are then almost three years old. With the launch of the new product another segment of the market is opened up. In the vast majority of instances this segment is smaller than the existing core business of the company, so the new product does not benefit from any scale economies. If the new product slices a segment out of the company's existing products it will even damage the economies of those products as they will then have a smaller volume base. The probability of offering the consumer an attractive value-for-money offer becomes very small, especially since, on top of the company's own relatively speaking more expensive production, the retailers will take their larger margins.

This classical NPD process leaves the company vulnerable on their core business and the old products are milked to the benefit of the new.

The next phase is almost inevitable: as the volume of core, profitable, business declines, more resources are poured into new ventures to make up for the losses on the 'old' ones. The cycle repeats itself, sales become even more fragmented and the profits deteriorate even further. We have a negative cycle of expensive launches and fragmenting sales (Figure 12.1 opposite).

I have deliberately exaggerated the implications of the current NPD process. In reality things are not quite as bad because most companies are managed by intelligent people with a lot of business sense, but the opportunities for a more efficient operation are indicated.

The value-added marketing approach to NPD

The value-added marketing approach to NPD is different in that the time-scale is more compact as there is less reliance on market research, only truly new products are launched and the new products have to offer a significantly better value for money. It is

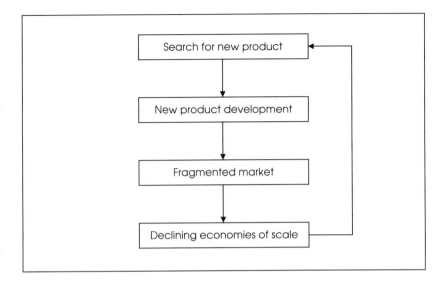

Figure 12.1 The negative NPD cycle

similar in that, in principle, a new product creates a new segment in the market. The new product is offering something new and better, and provided that the consumers value the produce as intended, a new market segment is opened up.

The greater emphasis on existing products with OPD does not mean that one can afford to ignore new products. There will always be new opportunities; customers' views and attitudes change, as in the case of Timotei; and there are still many new technological breakthroughs to come. They will just happen less often.

The main elements for NPD success are as follows:

1 Balance the NPD activities with old product development.

2 Use the technological innovations on new *and* old products.

3 Launch new products only when there really is an opportunity to achieve a better perceived value with the customers.

The consequences of these statements on NPD activities are, firstly, proper development resources have to be deployed to improve existing products and, secondly, even though increased focus is put on existing business, new product development cannot be neglected.

NPD and OPD become very similar in the context of value-added marketing. The difference is only that one is based on an existing concept or product, and the other is created from scratch.

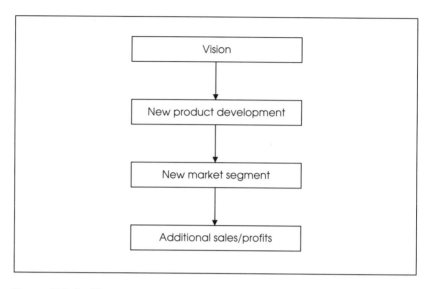

Figure 12.2 Positive new product development

New products derive either from a vision of an opportunity in the future (filling a gap) or from a technical breakthrough making a 'familiar' vision come true. In the former case, the process is very similar to classical marketing with the important difference that the implementation time will be shorter (Figure 12.2).

The search process is made shorter as market research can seldom be used successfully to find new market opportunities. On the other hand, it is always possible to check a new product with customers to evaluate its acceptance, although even that, if it is done too early in the process and too soon before a potential launch date, is a fairly useless exercise. A concept is easy to grasp if you are working in marketing; it is more difficult for a customer and, above all, a statement of intent today is not valid in 12–18 months' time. Eliminating 'insurance-research' and substituting solid market know-how and experience quickens the process. Some of the lessons learned from Japan, described in Chapter 4, may be applied.

Reducing the amount of pre-launch research, however, is not a licence for 'gut feel' marketing. The difference between making decisions on the basis of market know-how and making them on the basis of 'gut feel' is that the former is founded on experience of a specific market segment while the latter is an instinct dependent on personal experience. 'Gut feel' marketing can be extremely dangerous as it is very easy to lose touch with reality.

In both NPD and OPD the *vision* is important, although the creative requirement is higher in NPD. The market variables are less well known and, by definition, everything is 'new'. It is necessary to formulate a vision that substantially exceeds the expectations of the consumers. It has to be several years ahead of what the customers think is feasible.

A prerequisite for a NPD programme is that resources are allocated to research and development. This is necessary if a company wishes to stay ahead, otherwise the old products will be old in the full sense of the word and new products will not materialize. On the other hand, NPD is no different from the other parts of the marketing mix, in that a well-organized project is not significantly more expensive than a poor one. According to Booz, Allen & Hamilton, the consultants, the companies with a successful R&D track record do not spend more on development, as a percentage of sales, than the unsuccessful ones. It is not what you spend, it is how you spend it.

The illustrative example of the demise of the western motorcycle industry is well known. The disappearance of that industry was certainly at least partly due to a product development strategy that was inferior. The Japanese product was not only cheaper, it was of a better quality and was easier to handle.

Another case, just as dramatic, was the almost total disappearance of the Swiss watch industry. The Swiss did not realize that they had to develop, and sell, products that were technologically contemporary. The result was that the old industry of mechanical watches disappeared almost overnight because of the superiority of the electronic watch. The Swiss case gives another lesson: it is not enough to invent, you have to apply.

The Swiss invented the crystal that made it possible to have a cheap, accurate watch, but they did not see the opportunities that the new invention held! This is very similar to the tale of Sony and the VCR, discussed in an earlier chapter. It was not until many years later, with the launch of the Swatch, that the Swiss watch industry recovered.

NPD and quality

The tangible product values are the foundation of the marketing programme. By placing the focus on the achievement of improved perceived values, the NPD work becomes more specific and better targeted. The new products must really offer a clear improvement in perceived tangible values over competition.

Classical marketing has ignored this to the detriment of a number of industries. In the latest edition of P. Kotler's classical marketing textbook, a complete chapter of 40 pages is devoted to new product development. Two sentences refer to product quality.

Just as with existing products, the perceived quality of a new product is crucial to its ability to succeed. The Japanese 'wave' has to a large extent been based on quality, and constant improvement of the quality in its widest sense.

'Me-too' products

Value-added marketing, if correctly applied, should also definitely stop any 'me-too' product launch. By definition, a product that is similar to one that is already available on the market (a 'me-too') does not offer the customers a better perceived value, so it should not be considered for a launch. The customers have already a certain amount of confidence in the existing product (the one that is being copied), and obviously rate it to such a degree that they buy it. If the new product does not offer something that is substantially better, there is no justification for its inclusion in the product portfolio.

If, for a number of years, you have bought your greengroceries from one specific trader on the market, you will only try a new supplier if this new supplier really has something better to offer: better quality, better supplies, wider assortment, and so on. In other words, the perceived attractions of any new business have to be strong enough to tempt the customers away from their usual source of supplies.

The situation in the vegetable market is no different from other types of market. If a new marmalade is to succeed, it has to be perceived as better; if a new car is to succeed it has to have something that makes it superior to the other models.

Of the estimated 12 000 new food items that were launched in western Europe and North America last year, how many really offered a better perceived value for money than the current products?

The only successful approach for new products is where the emphasis is on producing products that are not only new but are also better. A quantitative evaluation of the perceived value of the proposed projects will make the whole NPD exercise one that will deliver a more profitable output for the company.

Ferrero's successful NPD

Ferrero is probably the most successful confectionery company in Europe. In the UK it is best known for the golden wrapped chocolate/almond pieces in the transparent box.

EXAMPLE Ferrero is an Italian privately held company with a turnover in 1989 of 3000 billion Italian lira (approx £1.4 billion), making it the third largest food company in Italy. Ferrero has had a string of original, creative product launches (in addition to the golden box) during the 1980s, such as Kinder Surprise, Tic Tacs and Raffaello. Because of the thoroughness with which Ferrero approaches the market, and the deep understanding the company has of the consumers in different European countries, the success rate has been extremely impressive. The number of new product introductions have been kept low, but all aspects of the quality have in all cases been superior. The company has in particular been successful in defining interesting and attractive product concepts, as well as making sure that virtually each new concept has represented a technological breakthrough. In that way they have not only created a strong position by giving the customer a very attractive perceived value, they have also built a barrier of entry for any competitor who would like to copy.

In the marketing programmes they are constantly evaluating new, alternative ways of selling the products and building know-how of how the marketplace works. It has also been noted by a number of observers that the major reasons behind its success are that the company is private (no short-term pressures from the stock market) and has not been involved in any major acquisitions (so it has been able to concentrate on what it knows best).

Mars' successful NPD

Each year, British retail trade magazine *Supermarketing* publishes the grocery trade's judgement on which of the new products launched that year, the trade regards as being most successful. An analysis of the last five years' top three in the survey confirms the value-added marketing principles. Some of the *Supermarketing* winners have been concepts that has given the customer a 'better mouse-trap'; on other occasions the top items have offered better product values *and* strong value-building communication.

EXAMPLE 1 In 1987 the winner was Tracker from Mars. The product concept was not new as müsli bars were already on the market, but Mars' execution of the concept was excellent. The Mars Company's explanation of the reason for the success was 'Mars Confectionery believed it could make a better tasting, more satisfying product, which would still be full of good natural ingredients.' Tracker quickly became one of the top 10 confectionery count lines, which is proof enough of the Mars belief.

Another example is the Mars ice-cream bar. This product proves the point that if the product is right from a perceived value point of view, the customer will buy even if the unit price is high.

EXAMPLE 2   The ice-cream bar was launched in Europe in April 1989 and was an instant success. It became the top selling item in the freezer cabinets of at least one of the major retail chains in the UK only six months after launch, and in the 1990 ice-cream season challenged the top selling item (Wall's Cornetto at £50 million per annum) for market leadership. The success is based on a combination of the wide appeal of the Mars bar, the second most popular count line in the UK, and the attraction of impulse ice-cream items, which in the UK is an area starved of real innovation. The product is not cheap – distinctly premium priced at 2–3 times the price of the chocolate bar – but it has proved to have very strong initial attraction and satisfaction values. The repeat purchase rate is ensured by a high-quality product make up, very similar to the count line, and the use of only the best quality ingredients. In March 1991 the Mars Confectionery Company could proudly advertise across the UK trade press that Mars ice-cream is the best selling ice-cream in the UK.

An extra twist to the Mars story is that the success was universal across Europe.

Conclusion

Product development resources must be allocated so that an existing product's need for improvement does not suffer from over-emphasis on new products. New technology can be used not only to make new products, but also to reformulate the existing ones.

To be successful new products not only have to be different, they have to be noticeably better. Any new concept must offer a superior quality and at the same time represent something new. The Ferrero products as well as the Mars ice-cream example illustrate this principle. When existing products are of an inferior quality it is feasible to launch a product based only on superior quality, such as the Tracker.

All proposals for new products must be judged against a background of the potential perceived value balance and how strong the total offer is in comparison with the competition. If a product does not promise to deliver a superior value perception, then it is better not to launch it and save the resources. If a new product is being considered for launch, it should be perceived by the ultimate customer as significantly better than existing products.

13

Making it easier to use the product

For customer satisfaction nothing can replace solid product performance values. That is the basis for value-added marketing. It is, however, only the beginning. There are many opportunities to add value to a product after it has been designed and manufactured. With most products it is possible to improve the 'software': such things as usage instructions, preparation instructions and the organization's ability to give service.

These types of activities are often quite inexpensive and flexible, involving only creation and printing. It is also frequently an area that is overlooked and is relegated to the most junior staff as many consider it to be a less sophisticated form of marketing. This is false, a comparison with a computer is valid: just as a computer will do nothing useful without software, a product without instructions is quite useless.

A strong position in this area has several advantages.

1 It adds perceived value by making the usage of the product easier.

2 If the 'software'/information is better than that from the other companies, that in itself will give the product a relative advantage.

3 The information that is given with the product can induce the customer to use the product in more ways than originally envisaged.

An additional positive effect from a company's point of view with this type of 'software', with the exception of after-sales-service and similar activities, is that it is a cheap way of enhancing the value of the product. The cost/benefit effect on the perceived value balance becomes very positive.

The way these opportunities are handled will reflect on the customers' general impression of the company. It is quite reasonable for a customer to assume that if a company does not know how to inform people of its products, then it is not particularly good at what it does in general.

The easiest way to investigate the potential for improvement is to play the part of a new customer. There are few alternatives to the principle of acquiring knowledge through the use of a product. Go into a shop, buy the product, take it home, use it following the instructions, and make a note of the process. The result of such a simple survey will trigger a number of suggestions for change.

Make the usage easier

The usage instructions are a classical, often neglected, part of the FMCG marketers' marketing mix. Everything from a pack of fish fingers to a Porsche sports car comes with usage instructions. To take the more humble example of the two, it costs as much to print an obscure cooking instruction on a pack of fish fingers as it does to print one that is easy to follow. The printing costs are identical, the only difference is that to give clear instructions you need more time and more experience. It takes time to perform all the cooking trials that are necessary to ensure that the instructions given are the best, but the effort is insignificant in relation to the disappointment and lost repeat sales that a wrong instruction can cause.

The effort to make sure that the instructions are written in an easily understood style is something that requires effort and discipline, but no more than for most other activities. The instructions are certainly more important for the perception of a product than the copy in an advertisement. The former is perhaps read by 30 per cent of the target group, the latter by 5 per cent.

The efforts in this area can move beyond the general minimum. To give more value to the product, the amount of information can be extended. In the case of fish fingers it can cover not only the traditional ways of preparing the product, but also how to prepare the fish fingers in an oven.

It will take more time and effort to determine the right way to prepare it but, as above, the effort in determining the correct way is much less than the possible disappointment and devaluation a wrong cooking instruction can cause. The fish example is used because it is simple, but speaking as a consumer rather than as a marketing manager, some companies have many improvements to make before the opportunities are exhausted.

The example above refers to a simple and common product, but the issue is more complex and more important when dealing with capital goods. The instruction booklet for a car or a home computer can make the new owner happy or frustrated. This initial reaction is bound to affect his or her future relations with that investment and, consequently, the repeat purchase rate. If the instructions are complicated and difficult to understand, the owner might never discover some of the features the manufacturer has built into the equipment. In this area the normal FMCG companies are far ahead of the electronics industry. Most instruction books or files I have at home are just too technical and too difficult to understand. For instance, I have a JVC video recorder; an excellent recorder, but it took me several hours to master the controls and I still discover new features after using the machine for over six months because the user's manual is virtually inaccessible.

Making the usage instructions clearer, for example, will improve both the attraction and the repeat purchase rate. The first glance at a product is likely to include the on-pack information, the usage instructions. As a customer you do not want to buy something that you do not understand how to use. So the attraction, the first purchase, is influenced.

The repeat purchase rate is directly influenced by how easy it is to use the product at home. Will the usage instructions make it possible for the customer to get the maximum benefit from the product? If the customer discovers that the fish fingers are half frozen after following the instructions, then that is unlikely to be an incitement for a repeat purchase. The frustration over the inaccessibility of technical features on a VCR will not encourage anyone to recommend the brand to a friend.

The frequency of purchase can also be increased by providing additional information that will help the customer to use the product in ways other than 'normal'. If the fish finger pack also carries a few serving suggestions and recipes, that might help the consumption rate.

There are several examples in the FMCG business of how this has been done with great success. One such example comes from Campbell's condensed soups. As a method of promoting their range of soups and giving them a high perceived culinary value, Campbell's have, in several European markets, had a consistent policy of promoting the use of their soups in recipes. Rather than just suggesting that a soup should be made of the contents, the can label has carried information on how to use the condensed soup as an ingredient in casseroles, sauces, etc. The culinary impression, value, has been enhanced and the frequency of usage has increased.

Another example of extending the usage of a product, is the Lea & Perrin case which won the company and its advertising agency the *Marketing* award for innovation at the 1990 IPA advertising effectiveness awards. Lea & Perrin's Worcestershire Sauce is one of those products that many are aware of but few people buy, and those who do often use only small amounts. The campaign that got the award in 1990 featured various ways in which the sauce could be used as a cooking aid. The result of the first phase of the campaign, which was regional and thus measurable against the rest of the country, was that the sales increased by 32 per cent, and advertising recall research indicated that the versatility message was the main factor behind the sales growth. In the Lea & Perrin case, advertising was used to communicate the sauce's versatility. The message could just as well have been communicated via the label or a leaflet. The conclusion is that the core message, versatility, is relevant and if properly communicated it will increase sales.

The 'software' will improve the perceived value, not only by making the traditional way of using the product better or easier and by giving suggestions for alternative uses, but also by portraying the manufacturer as a more knowledgeable and caring company. The 'software' should always be regarded as a significant part of the marketing mix as it gives an excellent perceived customer value return on invested time.

Information

The best example of using general information as a means of achieving better perceived value is Kellogg's use of the back panel of their cereal packs. As all consumers of breakfast cereals know, the back of the pack is used for all kinds of purposes, everything from presenting consumer offers to providing information about such subjects as the 'animal kingdom', outer space or sports events. All this adds value to the product by giving interesting and/or useful information. The cost is small in relation to the caring image it creates, not to mention the entertainment value in making the breakfast less boring.

Kellogg's do have a practical advantage in that the cereal packs offer a large display area. That makes the process easier but it does not have to be a reason for not using this type of communication to enhance the product value.

Denmark is a country well known for its two main breweries, Tuborg and Carlsberg. Tuborg has for many years had in the home market a communication philosophy with plenty of character. One feature is the creative use of the label. Almost all brands of beer or lager have a main label and a neck label. For many years Tuborg has used the neck label as a way of giving the consumers interesting pieces of information, sometimes related to the drink, but mostly covering subjects with no apparent relationship with the brand. Beer is a social drink and an 'interesting fact' can provide the drinker with a subject for conversation.

After sales service

In the capital goods sector, after sales service represents an important part of enhancing the perceived value of the product. Few people would consider buying a car if they were not sure of having access to after sales service. The same applies to many other capital goods. After sales service organizations are often expensive to run, but, on the other hand, the cost of running a good organization is not dramatically higher than running a bad one. Needless to say, the best alternative is to have a product that requires no service at all.

After sales service is traditionally only considered in the context of the supply of capital goods, but it also has a role in FMCG markets. Most companies are aware of the fact that customer service can play an essential part in the relations between the producer and the retailer, but an opportunity also exists in producer–final consumer relations. Companies who have introduced 'consumer relations' telephone numbers, preferably freephone, have found that the consumers have many questions and like them to be answered. The display of a telephone number on a label or in an advertisement adds a 'caring' value to the brand, and if the telephone is answered in a pleasant way, then each customer calling in feels that little bit more loyal. How letters are answered is another small but potentially important way of building customer loyalty and a favourable impression, especially when the word of mouth/ multiplier effect is taken into account (see Chapter 18 on advertising).

The example of Volvo in Sweden was mentioned earlier. The Volvo network in Sweden is most impressive, consisting of a large number of dealers and garages providing a total national cover. The service network has over many years been an influential factor in creating positive consumer values. The professionalism of the participating garages plays a significant part in setting Volvo apart from its competitors.

This strong service organization influences both the attraction and over-satisfaction values:

1 As it is a dense national system the service is available when required, which gives confidence and security to the buyer. The attraction value of the Volvo car is influenced.

2 The standardized systems ensure that the car is well looked after, which is a benefit in itself but it also has a financial implication in that a well-maintained car retains its second-hand value. The repeat purchase rate is directly affected by the high second-hand value of the car.

The service organization is an impressive image-maker in itself, as it is well run, but it has also become a good money maker for the Volvo dealers through turnover and, in particular, the sales of spare parts. There is also an indirect effect in that, through visits to the dealer, the customer–supplier contact is maintained.

Conclusion

The opportunities of adding tangible benefits and value to a product through 'software' are often neglected. Part of the reason is that it has so far lacked the glamour that most marketers see in advertising. Another reason is that many brand managers have not had the necessary product knowledge to understand and implement programmes of this type. To be able to judge whether the information supplied with a product is sufficient, superior or inferior to that of the competitive products, you have to have a thorough understanding and knowledge of the product and the customers.

A comprehensive value-added programme should include efforts to:

• make the usage instructions easy to understand, whether the product is fish fingers or a computer

• make the information and the service organizations better than those of the competitors

• make sure that the information given is as comprehensive as possible, covering all the relevant aspects of the product.

Such a programme, although less important than improving the real product quality, will give the company an excellent return on the allocated resources, especially as most of the activities are inexpensive to implement.

14

Building intangible values

The intangible values have a significant impact on attracting and keeping a customer. It is almost impossible to attract a customer without having some intangible values connected with the product. It is the aura surrounding a product that will induce a consumer to select it in the supermarket. Similarly, a communication campaign, enhancing the perceived image of a product, can have a strong influence on the next purchase, swinging the buying decision in the direction of a specific product.

A decision to invest in improving the intangible values cannot be taken in isolation from an evaluation of the tangible values. The product in question must be of a good quality and the information that follows with the purchase must, equally, be of a high standard, otherwise there will be no success. Priority has to be given to ensuring that these factors are of a superior standing because it is wasteful to spend time and money trying to build an exciting image for a product if the base, the product, is of a poor quality. That will only result in disappointed customers, who will not make repeat purchases. Only travelling con-men can succeed with a business based on initial purchases only.

The tangible dimensions make up only half of the value side of the value balance. In a world of quick technological transfer, and when the risk for product imitation is high, a strong position regarding the intangible values is becoming more and more important.

In order to survive in the marketplace, and to be profitable, a company has to use all available means to create a strong perceived value-for-money proposition. The 'me-too' product policy of some competitors makes it essential to ensure that the communication programme is setting the product apart, in character and value, from the competition.

The process of adding intangible perceived values to a product is basically all about communication – i.e. communication as in advertising but also as in pack design, PR, personal selling and promotion.

The objectives with communication in value-added marketing are two-fold. It is a question of building values to attract the customers and then, post-purchase, enhancing the perceived value, the customer over-satisfaction, so that the repeat purchase rate stays high or increases.

Before going into the specific methods by which value-added marketing can be applied to a company's communication programme, we shall consider a few general aspects.

In virtually all business contexts, two factors are crucial to long-term success: consistency and relevance. These two factors are also very important in the process to improve the perceived value – the effect – of the communication programme.

Consistency

As always in marketing and communication, consistency across all the various activities makes the total greater than the sum of the parts. The message has to be consistent and executed in a way that shows the message to be a credible 'part' of the company or product, and not something that has been 'glued on' by a creative department.

Consistency in communication has two aspects.

1 The message should be similar across all media; the imagery has to bear a resemblance; and the copy platform must be understood as coming from the same organization. The brand or product identity has to be respected and honoured.

2 The message has to be consistent with the product. The intangible values have to be in harmony with the tangible product benefits.

This does not mean, however, that the message has to be identical in all instances. The core message can have a full spectrum of different expressions, each designed for a specific occasion or audience.

Consistency is important because if the communication creates confusion with the recipient of the message(s), that confusion in itself will devalue not only the effect of the message but also the product. After all, who wants to buy something from someone who does not know what they are doing, cannot explain the product, or does not know what the products of the company stand for.

The street trader who makes claims about certain products and then cannot answer the most basic questions from the customers on how the produce is grown or how to prepare it has a credibility problem and is unlikely to be trusted. Similarly, the trader is also unlikely to be successful if, one day, his or her potatoes are said to be good only for baking and the next day are recommended for making chips. That would make the customers wonder, not only about the trader's ability, but also about the quality of the merchandise.

Relevance

The message a company communicates in order to enhance the product has to be relevant. If a message is not within the value spectrum of a chosen customer group, the effect will be insignificant. The potential customers will just ignore the message and the whole communication process will not generate a positive effect. In an extreme situation, the customers might even take offence. In that case the result becomes one of a decrease, rather than increase, of the perceived value. Only someone who is aware of what the customers think and do can make a proper decision as to which message is relevant and which is not. There is no substitute for thorough market and customer knowledge. Market research is, of course, an option but research has a number of shortcomings such as speed and cost, and one cannot, after all, research everything.

Conclusion

Consistency and relevance apply to all parts of the marketing mix. In the hardening battle for market share, the message(s) and the product(s) have to be projected as solidly as possible.

15

Branding

The value of a brand is not something that one can easily change. Although it is not a part of the marketing mix, but an effect of it, the subject has nevertheless been included as branding plays an essential role in the communication process, denoting the identity of the product or service.

While branding can almost make or break a product, it has to be looked at in proportion to its role. *The customer buys a product, not a brand*. The physical purchasing action is caused by a decision to acquire a product; the brand is there to serve as a means of identifying the manufacturer. The values of the brand will reflect on the product, but one must not forget that it is the product that is bought.

The brand imagery can reinforce product values – and often does so quite significantly – and turn people into customers as well as enhance product satisfaction. The customers' objective, however, is to buy a product and the quality experience (over-satisfaction, or not) of that product is what will entice them to make, or not make, a second purchase. The product reflects on the brand as much as the brand reflects on the product.

The expression that 'the customer buys a brand' is not only logically wrong, it is conceptually wrong and can lead marketers to believe that product quality is less important, assuming that creating the 'right' kind of imagery will overcome potential deficits in tangible product values.

One must relate branding to how the customer sees it, more than how the marketer, or perhaps the City analyst, would like to see it.

Branding as an expression is used in two different senses, but only one of those will be considered. Firstly, branding is about the ability of a brand to give value to a product and the creation of those values connected to the brand. Secondly, branding is also used to cover the activities related to the creation of a visual identity – i.e. activities such as ensuring that all parts of the communication have a consistent 'face' and that the visual properties are correctly used from a communication as well as a legal point of view. My analysis of branding in this chapter is exclusively concerned with branding in the first sense: that of creating value.

It is important not to confuse the two expressions. Many companies have excellent communication branding, where all visual elements in all possible contexts are totally consistent with a strong visual identity. That is not a guarantee for an efficient branding/value process as the success of that depends on the contents of the brand(s). If the brand has no value to give to the customers, it does not mean anything; the beautiful communication is of very little use. It is far better to be in a position where the brand has credibility with the customers but the communication is unclear. A skilled design consultant can deal quickly and adequately with such a problem as there is a value base on which to build.

The origins of branding

To understand how a brand can be used by a marketer, it is useful to look at how the customers, the consumers, look at a brand and how branding first started. Originally, branding was used to identify property: cattle was branded (literally and conceptually) so that each person knew who owned which cow.

The first example of branding, as a means of identifying a manufacturer, goes back to pre-Roman civilizations, where clay 'lamps' were marked to facilitate the identification of specific artisans or towns producing high-quality goods. Various methods of branding have been used through the ages, such as the hallmarking of metals and watermarking of paper. The rise in the trade of consumer goods in the nineteenth century gave branding an extended role. The long distances between the makers and the users of products, and the proliferation of manufacturers and goods, made it necessary – especially for the quality producers of the time – to establish a method by which their goods could easily be identified. In an anonymous world with, on the face of it, similar goods it was impossible to build a quality reputation without a means of identification: branding.

Historically the brand represented the manufacturer, the artisan. The goods were branded so that the customer knew where they came from. That information helped the customer to evaluate whether the product was worth having, prior to purchase. The brand was synonymous with the producer, and that was the basis for having a brand.

In the world of today the role of the brand is the same, and in most instances that is why a brand is used and how it is understood by the consumers.

The brand *symbolizes* the maker of the product. Even in cases where it is fairly obvious that the brand is not a manufacturer, such as 'Yorkie', 'Bounty' or 'After Eight', the instant reflection of the customer – that the brand is the symbol of the maker – has been developed into the brand representing a specific type of product from the manufacturer in question. That makes the brand not only the symbol for a company, but also the carrier of expectations of specific qualities, such as a certain taste, price level or product category.

That symbolism is also what makes a sub-brand a relevant concept. A sub-brand is a symbol of a range of products that share certain characteristics, and comes from a specific company (=brand). The words Findus Lean Cuisine on a pack tells a customer that the products carrying that brand/sub-brand are all low in calories, of a high quality, and have a certain taste profile. The Findus brand on the pack indicates that it is a frozen product, because that is what the brand is known to represent, and the values connected to the brand tell the customer that the product is made by a trusted company.

It is necessary to fully understand this symbolism because the person in charge of a brand, whether it is big or small, is the one that plays the role of 'manufacturer' for the customer. The brand 'owner' is the one who guarantees that the product is of a certain standard. If the brand is handled by a brand manager, then it is that person who must feel the responsibility; if the brand is controlled by the marketing director, then he or she is the one who has to carry the role of the producer.

If the brands are looked at from this traditional and 'product-led' angle, the way companies should treat their brands becomes much more understandable and easy to follow. Brands must be nurtured and, just as successful artisans take great pride in their work, each company must take care of how its 'work' reflects on that company's symbol, the brand. True artisans are very careful with their reputations and maintain a standard of work that makes them proud; but, more importantly, if it also makes the customers happy they will return with more business and may recommend those artisans to other people.

Successful branding

Products carrying a specific brand have to be handled with the same concern as the artisans show in their work. All activities that take place under the umbrella of a brand add to or subtract from the value. The customer's evaluation of a brand is a result of all the experiences that the customer has had of products with that brand, or, more precisely, what the customer remembers of those experiences. That includes products, services, personal contacts, advertising, promotions, 'word of mouth', etc.

This mix of perceptions, 'memories', which are built up over a long time, makes the brand potentially the most powerful giver of intangible perceived values. After all, a customer's first interest prior to purchasing a product is 'who has made it'. If that 'person' (i.e. the brand) has a good reputation, it gives the customer confidence to buy the product.

While the brand can be the most powerful communicator of value, it is also the one that the marketer can do the least with in a direct sense, because the brand's image is the sum of the activities of the past.

From an operational point of view, a company should be very careful when and how a brand is used. If a 'good' brand is used for poorly perceived products, the brand will be devalued. If a company repeats that on a number of product launches, the brand will lose much of its power to give a positive intangible perceived value. On the other hand, if the new products are perceived as good, the value of the brand will increase.

During the latter part of the 1980s when there were a number of major take-overs, the value of brands was a major discussion point (and the accounting principles are still unresolved). The intangible value of brands was the, rightful, justification for many high-priced deals. When the Nestlé Company acquired Rowntree-Mackintosh in 1989 at over four times the value of the assets, they paid for the value of the brands. In reality, though, the acquisitors did not pay for the brands as such. What they bought was a reputation – the trust that many customers held with the brands in question. The crucial conclusion of this argument is that if the trust is subsequently misused, the value of the brands will disappear and in due course will be deemed worthless.

As an extreme example, if the Rolls-Royce Car Company was to launch an inferior model carrying the famous RR badge, its reputation would take a serious knock. If it were to be repeated, the value of the brand would soon drop. That was what happened to Jaguar in the 1970s, as poor workmanship ruined the reputation of one of the world's most famous car brands to the extent that sales suffered dramatically. Only with a new chief executive, John Egan, and a total commitment did the company survive, and it did it so well that the Ford Motor Company was prepared to pay a large amount of money to gain access to the brand.

Another aspect of branding is 'leveraging/stretching brand strengths', a technique that has grown quite popular over the last few years. The expression stands for using a familiar brand in a company's portfolio on a product outside the original market. The previously described Mars ice-cream is the perfect example of a well-executed stretching of brand values. Such an exercise is only successful when the process makes sense in the eyes of the consumer. The main reason for using a familiar brand across more categories is to make the advertising budgets go further. This will only work if the various product categories and the product quality are consistent with each other, such as in the case of Mars ice-cream. The ice-cream bar is a perfect reflection of the core Mars bar brand values, as well as being in a market conceptually close to that of chocolate count lines. If a well-known brand is used across too many new items from product areas that are inconsistent with the 'home' of the brand, the logo will have very little positive effect. If the process is repeated, the reputation of the brand will be dented and the brand's ability to endorse a product will diminish.

Marks & Spencer is an excellent example of building brand strengths and understanding that the reputation of a brand rests with the product quality. Over many years this retail organization has sold products that have had an excellent perceived value. This value perception has rubbed off on the brand so that today, almost regardless of product category, the British public has an enormous confidence in St Michael products and will willingly pay a premium price for them. The St Michael brand power has been built with no spend on advertising but with a tremendous amount of effort in other areas, such as product formulation, quality control, range policy, staff training and customer dialogue. The Marks & Spencer management principles are legendary in all these areas.

Branding is about how a company can use its identity or identities with the customers to increase the perceived value of its products. The ability of the brand to endorse a product depends on how and to what extent positive values have been accumulated over time.

The word 'branding' is used quite carelessly and it usually refers to displaying the brand as clearly as possible. Successful branding is

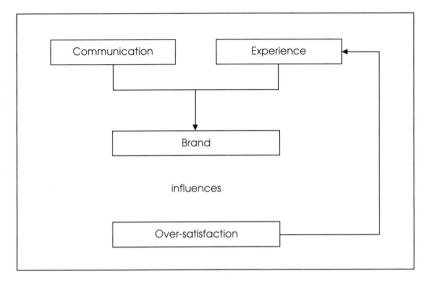

Figure 15.1 Creation of brand values

something different: it is (1) to ensure that the products that carry a certain brand have a superior value-for-money perception with the key customer groups and (2) to use that perception to identify the origins of products and thus strengthen the value, as well as the credibility, of the communication.

The brand perception can be based on real product over-satisfaction *as well as* communication (Figure 15.1). It is possible to have a very high regard for a product without ever having used it, very few people have owned a Rolls-Royce or even ridden in one, but most people think very highly of a car with the RR badge.

Corporate advertising

A subject that is closely related to branding is 'corporate advertising', which is understood to be non-product related advertising. It is not range advertising, as a range is a number of products that have a strong common denominator, and range advertising is fundamentally the same as product advertising.

It is sometimes suggested that corporate advertising is an economical way of building sales. It is said to be 'economical' because, with one message, it can theoretically cover a number of products, ranges and brands. Unfortunately, corporate advertising is generally speaking not a good idea. To advertise the corporation instead of the product is to start with the concept that is furthest from the purchased item. The customer buys a product, not a corporation, therefore it is the value of the product that primarily needs to be enhanced. That can most efficiently be done through product communication. The product and the communication builds the perceived value, which reflects initially on the brand and then on the corporation.

By starting with the corporation, the communication process is being done in reverse order. The communication becomes less relevant to the customer, who is primarily interested in the product (or service), not the corporation.

If the object of the advertising is to enforce a position with the stock market or a distribution network, and is not directly related to the sale of products to the consumers, the method and relevance change, but not the logic. For the stock market, the corporation is the product and, as such, is the one that must be promoted and whose value has to be enhanced. For the distributive trade, the corporation might very well be playing the role of the brand, and as such corporate advertising might be a useful concept for that specific target group.

The best corporate advertising is excellent products (such as from M&S), with excellent staff, service and product communication.

Conclusion

The brand is a part of all types of communication. It is used in advertising, pack design and promotions. The power of the brand is not restricted to any type of communication.

Branding is a sensitive issue that has to be handled with great care. The brand represents the reputation of a company, those values that have been built up over years of product usage and exposure to advertising. The power of the brand can be increased by excellent products and decreased by poor products. A good brand can never rescue a poor product, but a poor product can damage a good brand. As the power of the brand to enhance the value of products lies in its history, each decision to change the branding philosophy of a company needs to be taken with caution.

A brand that has a strong position with customers can be an extremely powerful enhancer of the value of a product, as most customers place great importance on the origins of the products they purchase.

16

Design

The concept of design has received increasing attention over the past 10 years. Design awards have been introduced and the visual impact is discussed as never before. Most of these types of design discussions refer to industrial design, shop design or design in the sense of creating new clothes or furniture.

Design as a discipline made a great impact on the business world in the 1980s. The retail revolution of the previous decade would not have happened had it not been for the newly acquired ability to create attractive shopping environments.

Design in a FMCG marketing sense is equally a necessary prerequisite for success. The design is the most apparent part of most products. It is what the customer sees before, during and after a purchase. A product that is not properly designed, whatever the definition of that expression, is unlikely to get beyond the trade buyer's desk.

Virtually all the information a customer has before a 'first' purchase is generated from two sources: communication and/or the visual impression of a pack, the design. In reality, the pack design is in most instances the only direct line of communication between a producer and the customers. Of, perhaps, 10 000 items in an average supermarket, only a minority are advertised brands, and, of those, only a handful are backed by sufficient resources and creative capacity to achieve really memorable advertising.

The pack, and its visual impression, follows the product through its 'life' in the home of the customer. Many products are kept in their containers, which are sometimes used frequently, like a jar of marmalade, and sometimes less so, like soap. The visual impression needs to be memorable if the product is to be bought again. An easily remembered product design obviously makes it more likely that a high repeat purchase rate will be maintained.

The pack design not only creates an impact for all types of products, but it has a much wider spectrum of influence than media communication.

On the basis of the multi-dimensional impact of pack design it is not a particularly controversial statement to conclude that, in the FMCG business, the pack design is the most important part of the communication mix.

'Design' in this context is the 'outside' of a product. In the supermarket it means the way the pack looks on the shelf; in a service industry it means what, for example, the restaurant looks like from outside and from inside. For a capital goods company it is related to whatever the customer sees before actually using the product. For the car it is the design of the body; for the typewriter it is the shell.

The visual impression of a product is of universal importance. Products with large advertising budgets can also make an impact via media, but for all the other products creating attraction at the point of sale is the only chance the producer has to influence and communicate with potential and current customers. By implication, it is obvious that an investment in pack design is the first area one should look at when evaluating the various ways of enhancing the intangible values. It is of general importance, and great emphasis should be given to it. Correctly executed, a reasonable investment can have a dramatically positive effect on the perceived value balance.

The two communication dimensions

In the communication process at the point of sale, the pack design has to fulfil a number of functions, but the most important are that the pack must transmit factual information and convey emotional values.

The most basic of these is that it has to give *information* regarding the product. In most cases, it is impossible to inspect the contents of a pack in the shop, therefore the outside of the product has to describe and explain the product. In addition to the basic information, the pack must also, as far as possible, describe the tangible benefits of the product.

In theory, the communication of the strictly functional characteristics of the product should add no perceived extra value. The reality is different; all types of communication carry an intangible value dimension. There is even an extra value connected to communicating the information in a manner that is clear and easily understood. Many purchases, especially in a supermarket, are made semi-automatically and often under great pressures of time. Such purchases are not the result of a thorough evaluation and, consequently, clear and easily recognizable product information is not only to the advantage of the customer but also transmits a positive feeling.

It is not only marketing people who show great interest in the on-pack information. The concern that legislative powers show for what is written on the pack is a sign of its importance. In most countries it is the most regulated part of the communication process, at least on food products.

In the primary communication, when customers consider the product the first time, the product's tangible values have priority. If the customers do not know what the product is, they will not buy it. This does not mean that the pack has to be loaded with (too much) information. It means that the relevant information – the information that customers primarily would like to see – has to be easily accessible. The design must communicate the basic product facts.

It is the other communication dimension – i.e. the opportunities to convey emotional values, enhancing the perceived value, in combination with the factual information – that opens up the possibilities of making the pack design a very powerful part of the marketing mix.

Everything from the product description to the product illustration can be used to enhance the *emotional value*. In classical marketing one is supposed to position the product through the pack design, and the design has to reflect the aspirations of the target group. That is a perfectly reasonable assumption; positioning is an excellent tool for clarifying the communication objectives. It is more significant, however, that the marketer should be aware of which communication values gives the pack the best commercial impact. The intangible values selected for the product must form the base of the positioning and the pack design.

There are several avenues for selecting interesting dimensions. The design can easily add value to the product through giving an impression of cheerfulness, nostalgia or whatever dimension is appropriate. It can make the product aspirationally 'classy'. It can make it representative of country values (such as Hovis bread), traditionalism (beer), or internationalism (Benetton's united colors). The supermarket shelves are full of examples, from a banal bag to luxurious, elaborate cartons.

The most basic approach of these alternatives, and also intellectually perhaps the most creative way of building a strong perceived value with a specific part of the consumer universe, is the generic design concept that was launched about 15 years ago. The generic products were unbranded, usually in plain white cartons, with just a straightforward product description. By discarding the overt emotional values, it created a new value (still based on emotions) of plainliness and no fuss and frills, which at least for a while held a great appeal.

At the other end of the scale are the top brands in the cosmetics business, where the pack design traditionally has played a major role in the marketing mix. The factual information is minimal, but the emotional impact and identity are maximized. All possibilities are used to create the desired emotional values.

The factual and emotional values have to complement each other, and no pack design is successful unless both dimensions are handled with the greatest respect.

Although pack design is the only option open to many marketers to communicate the benefits of a product, it is also very cost effective. The costs are of two types: the printing (or moulding in the case of bottles and jars) and the creation. It is only the creative cost that will increase if the standard of the design communication is increased, as it costs approximately as much to print a poor design as a good one. The creative cost can be quite high, but if the result is good it is money well spent. Compared to other communication techniques the cost/benefit effect on the value balance is very positive.

A few general comments

To be able to add value to a product through the design discipline, all the traditional communication 'rules' have to be applied. The information requirements must be well considered, the illustrations must be appropriate, the overall as well as the specific messages must be clear, the legal situation must be understood, and so on. To do this successfully, all the knowledge the marketer can muster of his customers, the product and the marketplace needs to be utilized.

An effective design has to reflect the product correctly. A new hair spray for young people must look very contemporary; a marmalade from Harrods should breathe tradition. The customer must get the impression that the design is consistent with the product, the message being consistent with the values the producer wishes to communicate.

Frequent customers have a visual memory of a product they buy. They will notice if the pack is changed and if the same product is displayed in both an old and a new design, they will probably buy the new one, as it will be considered more contemporary and fresher. If not, the new design is almost certainly not well executed. Managers with experience of changing pack design across a range know that the products with the old design will sell at a slower rate than those with the new one, everything else being equal.

Despite this, the design is the face of the product and, in a similar vein to tangible values, should not be changed too often or too radically. If changes are frequent the repeat purchase rate will suffer as the loyal customers may not find the product because they cannot recognize it, or may feel that it has changed too much and can no longer trust the contents.

Attraction and over-satisfaction

Because it is so often the only form of communication between a manufacturer and a potential customer, the design plays a dominating role when it comes to creating the appropriate value for a potential purchase. Excluding the (few) products where pull advertising builds attraction and enhances the product satisfaction, the design is the only 'voice' with which the producer can communicate with a potential customer. The design, with no help from any media, must create an impression that is so favourable that a potential customer is prepared to make a brand switch.

It should also be noted that even if the product in question is well known through several years of building repeat business or through heavy advertising, the importance of design does not diminish. Firstly, not every potential customer is exposed to advertising; and secondly, the effect of the advertising needs to be turned into sales, and the point of sale is where the design makes an impact. An easily recognizable pack with dimensions consistent with the advertising will enhance the totality.

Most products, new and old, are not advertised, so to generate trial it is essential for the pack to radiate the attraction dimensions of the product. These can span from the very basic (e.g. the product is a marmalade or an instant coffee) to the very emotional (e.g. this product will make you feel like a very attractive person). The design has to convey the basic essential facts clearly and concisely and the emotional values dramatically and powerfully.

Design is like clothes on a person; someone might be extremely pleasant and interesting, but if his or her dress and general appearance are totally unattractive, the number of people who would wish to make contact is likely to be very small. Similarly, few people will remember a person without character a week after their first meeting.

The identity, the design, is also important for repeat purchases of the product. There are two aspects of this point. Firstly, a design with a lot of character or with a unique graphic 'device' will help customers to find the product on the supermarket shelves and remind them of the (positive) values that they have experienced through the use of the product. Secondly, the impact of a good pack design goes beyond the store shelves. It will influence the repeat purchase rate since it can increase the satisfaction of a product throughout the time the product is in use in the home. The pack makes an impact all through the household. It is exposed to the customer throughout the entire shopping process – as it is carried home, as it is unloaded from the grocery bags, and as it is put into the fridge or the freezer. Perhaps it may also be used frequently while still in its original container. The pack design can continue to enhance the product value all through this sequence of events.

The change in consumption from butter, packed in a traditional paper or foil wrap, to the spreadable margarines, is an illustrative example. Butter, a traditional product of some age, usually comes in a type of packaging that must be discarded prior to usage on the breakfast table. The butter is transferred to a serving dish and the wrapper is discarded. On the other hand, the margarine comes in a functional, nice-looking tub, which can be used on the table. There is no need for a separate dish and the visual identity of the product stays with the consumer for each consumption occasion until the tub is empty. If it takes, on average, two weeks to consume a pack of butter or a tub of margarine, the last impression of the visual identity/brand of the butter is two weeks old by the time the repeat purchase is due, while the margarine customer probably saw the tub that same morning at breakfast. With the margarine tub the opportunities for a comprehensive communication are greater and the time span the design has to cover is much shorter. The repeat purchase rate is significantly more influenced by the design, and the possibilities to achieve a higher brand loyalty is greater, simply because of the shorter time span between seeing the product and buying a new one. Of course, the effect will only be to the brand's benefit if the product experience is positive.

A few examples of use of design

EXAMPLE 1   Kellogg's is probably the master of using pack design in an efficient way. The product benefits are clearly communicated, each pack has a personality, and the opportunities for giving extra information on the back and side panels are well utilized. Much of the product and brand loyalty for Kellogg's has been built at breakfast tables.

EXAMPLE 2   The Nescafé jar, which has been carefully designed to enhance both the tangible and the intangible values, is easy to open and close, and is constructed so that the aroma and delicacy of the product are protected. It also has a visual identity in the shape of the jar, which makes Nescafé easier to remember the next time coffee is purchased in the supermarket.

EXAMPLE 3   Johnson & Johnson's baby powder shows how one can use the shape of the pack to enhance the identity as well as make the product easier to use. J&J soon realized that a distinct design could be a very useful element in the marketing mix. The brand is far from new; the baby powder was introduced in 1893. In 1969 the traditional square bottle was discontinued and the 'waistline' bottle was introduced with a duel effect: it gave the product greater character and made it more recognizable; it also made the product easier to use. One tangible and one intangible effect of one fairly simple measure, a more distinct bottle.

Conclusion

The importance of pack design cannot be over-stated. A product can increase its perceived value by a large amount through a carefully and well-executed design. Conversely, a badly executed design represents lost opportunities.

Lost opportunities are always a potential danger as they will be grasped by competitors, but in the case of pack design there is the additional risk of damaging the brand values through recklessness. A deficient design will not only damage the product's own sales rate, it can also damage the reputation of the brand. Even if an individual does not intend to buy the specific product, the negative communication can reduce the brand value 'bank'. In addition, the pack design discipline is more controlled by the law enforcing authorities than any other part of the marketing mix. A legally unacceptable label can result in product recall.

The design can strongly influence the attraction values of a product. It is, in most cases, the only direct line of communication from the manufacturer to the consumers. Also, the repeat purchase rate can be improved by making the product better value, as Kellogg's have demonstrated. The quality of the design will certainly also make it easier or more difficult for the customer to find the product when a repeat purchase is required in the supermarket.

The pack design is the most important part of the communication mix. No other dimension gives the same opportunities to influence the purchase decision.

17

Sales promotions

Sales promotions of various shapes and forms is the traditional way of attempting to enhance the perceived value for money in the short-term perspective. The technique of offering the consumer something extra, whether it is a temporarily lower selling price or the opportunity to take part in a competition, theoretically improves the perceived value-for-money balance.

Unfortunately, most marketing people's experiences of promotions are that the period of the perceived value enhancement is quite brief and often expensive. The positive effect, the sales uplift, is short-lived and there is usually a slowdown of sales after the promotion, which reduces the gains that were made. Of course, it is very difficult to generalize as the customer expectations vary from business to business and from country to country. What one can say as a general comment is that the objective of 'all' promotions is to achieve short-term sales uplifts – in other words, an improved perceived value offer for a limited period.

Marketing managers have seldom been able to achieve

1 a planned increase in sales at a reasonable cost for the company

2 a sales effect that is not countered by a decline in sales in the following period

3 a sales uplift that does not harm the long-term perceived value of the product.

In 1, sales promotion programmes tend to use up a large proportion of the FMCG marketers' budgets. In recessional times in particular, the emphasis tends to switch to promotions, but often with very limited positive effect on the bottom line. In 2, the general experience of price promotions is that, with very few exceptions, sales during the period immediately following the promotion are well below average. This is not surprising as most loyal consumers will realize that the offer represents a bargain and will stock up for future use. The net result of such a consumption pattern is only a marginal increase in consumption (through in-home 'stock pressure'). In **3**, a classical non-price-related sales promotion will not damage the long-term perceived value, but a price-related promotion might do so.

Price-related promotions

There are many different types of promotional techniques and the most primitive of these is the price-off. This technique is as old as trading. The retail selling price is reduced by a certain percentage or amount over a specific period. The methods used to communicate this to the customers vary from a simple sign in the shop to elaborate advertising campaigns in the press, on the radio or on television. The strategy is that by lowering the price more customers will find the product attractive. This is often true, but is also often at the expense of future sales.

The perceived value-for-money balance gets a theoretical boost through the reduction in price. The perceived value remains the same but the cost declines. The consumers can react in three different ways to a price promotion. Which way a specific promotion will go depends, of course, on the type of product but also on what phase of introduction the product is in. Firstly, the consumer can look upon the promotion as a genuine offer, can take the opportunity to try the product, becomes converted and will buy the product again at a later date. This is the ideal situation; and if it does happen, it is usually with a new product that has excellent perceived tangible values. Secondly – which is probably the more common situation – the consumer looks upon the promotion as a short-term offer. In this case the ongoing value balance does not change as the offer is only available for a short period. The customer takes the opportunity to buy some extra items, with the result that sales decline after the promotion as people are using up the stocks in their homes. This type of promotion appeals to loyal consumers, but offers very limited scope for real sales increases because of the decline in sales after the promotion. As most of the extra sales are not eventually incremental but are made at a lower selling price, the accumulated profit might well be below average. The third alternative is relevant for products that are heavily and regularly promoted. The frequent promotions change the price perception and the consumers get used to a lower price. The promotional price becomes the standard price and the standard price becomes a temporary premium price. When the scheme is first introduced it is quite possible that a sales increase can be recorded as the increased perceived value for money might increase the customer base or the frequency of using the product. As to the ongoing business, the promotions become a necessity to maintain the price level where the product is selling in budgeted amounts, rather than a measure for achieving incremental sales.

The price-off promotional technique is full of pitfalls, but is nevertheless used extremely frequently. Its popularity stems from the fact that it is simple to implement and in many instances the retail trade is keen to have brand promotions to improve their perceived value as an inexpensive shop.

There are, however, situations in which the tactic with price cuts can be profitable. If the product is new, and it represents a large improvement over the competitors' products, a temporary low price might attract customers who otherwise would not have tried the product. The customer base will increase and the general sales level will improve. The situations in which this applies are quite few and an alternative might be to use the money to advertise the benefits or to lower the ongoing price on a permanent basis.

Another reason for the lack of real success with price promotions is that the promotional price change, usually around 10 per cent, is not enough to change the relative perceived value for money for the customer. The experience that it is difficult to achieve significant changes in the perceived value balance through price promotions is evidence of the fact that the perceived *value* of the product is more important than the *cost*. The retail trade in the UK, and especially J Sainsbury's and Marks & Spencer's, have understood this relationship. On the other hand, retail organizations in other countries, such as Germany and Sweden, still live in an era of focusing all their attention on achieving temporary low prices through frequent price promotions, instead of ensuring a long-term attractive value-for-money offer. The success of the former policy shows up in the profit and loss statement of these two UK retailers, both of whom have superior profitability records.

Price promotions are very common; there are very few FMCG businesses where temporary discounts are not a regular part of the promotional mix. The effect of the promotions is often illusive, because the temporary uplift in sales cannot be sustained. There are various reasons for this; for example, the relatively small price change does not influence the customers' value-for-money perception (it only influences the profit and loss statement through the lower per unit revenue).

There are situations in which a well-executed campaign can give positive short- and long-term results, but those occasions are rare and usually relate to new or infrequently purchased products.

Other sales promotion techniques

There are many other promotional techniques that are not price related. A supermarket survey will show examples of competitions, repeat purchase coupons, extra quantities of free product, self-liquidating offers, etc. All of these have been planned for a purpose, but they all share the same characteristics in that

- they are short term

- they often have a 'secondary' objective which, in reality, is more important than the consumer offer

- they are created by marketing departments who like to show that they are doing something

- they are demanded by sales departments who need something to talk to the customers about.

A promotion creates attention, but it does not really add any perceived value unless the offer is something that the customers will value, and those ideas are difficult to find. Most offers have a very low consumer pick-up, less than 5 per cent, and the direct sales effect will reflect that.

It is quite possible, however, that the secondary objective of the offer – i.e. to get the attention of the retailer – is fulfilled. The promotion will add value to the product for the supermarket buyer, instead of to the consumer. Such an objective, extra perceived value for the shop or the retail organization, can be a very reasonable concept for a company and one that justifies the expense and effort.

As to the third and fourth points above, many promotions are created for the simple reason that the marketing department felt the need to do something to highlight the product in the trade or in the salesforce. If that is the case the effort would be better spent trying to enhance the real perceived value of the product with the 'customer', whoever that may be, the consumer or the trade, so that a long-term future is secured for the product.

It would be foolish to assume that in today's FMCG world one could market a product without using promotional activities; the marketplace is too competitive. The non-price-related promotions offer much greater scope for value building than the price-related ones, which only affect the cost side of the balance. With a creative approach to the formulation of the promotions, one can combine the need to do something for the trade-customer with communicating a suitable message to the consumer-customer. Examples such as the Nescafé promotions featuring the offer of a red coffee mug and the

Kellogg's promotions where you can collect tokens on the Rice Krispies packs and receive a toy car (relevant for the target group) are certainly worth their costs.

The non-price-related promotions are easier to control from a financial point of view than the price-related ones. The effects of a non-price promotion are over when the closing date of the offer has past, while a price promotion can give negative effects for at least a month after the end of the promotion. If the price promotion is the first in a series that will result in the promotional price level being the normal one, it will mean that all future revenues might be deflated by 10 per cent. A very serious implication. A non-price promotion can also more easily be designed to take into account the perceived value profile of the product rather than the one-dimensional price promotion.

The real reason for promoting

The most general and common objective with arranging promotions is to create 'activity'. The seller uses the promotional marketing tool to create attention for his or her products in a crowded marketplace. The promotion becomes a communication technique rather than a tool for changing any perceived values. Correctly applied, the promotional activity can call on the attention of potential customers who will discover the (attractive) perceived values (without reference to any specific offer or price reduction) and buy. The noise level in today's FMCG markets is high and there are more different products than ever before on the shelves of the supermarkets. The marketer has to use several 'tricks' to cut through that noise level and a sales promotion activity is one. This communicative effect is more important than any change a promotion might bring to the perceived value balance.

As with other communicative marketing methods, the effort will be totally in vain if the perceived value falls short of expectations. If over-satisfaction is not achieved, the promotional expenses will be wasted and the money would have been much better spent on ensuring that the perceived value is superior to that of the competition.

Evaluation

In order to be effective in adding value to the products, the marketer must be realistic and look at the business as objectively as possible.

There are companies that have over years built up an effective system of promotional programmes. These companies use a consistent approach with similar techniques year after year and have been refining the offer each time to avoid the negative effects. A careful evaluation of the activities by the marketing and sales departments is one of the bases for the programme. Although this is easy to do, it is rarely done, and is often put at the bottom of the priority list. To get the benefit of the full process, promotion–evaluation–refining–evaluation, the marketers need to stay in their jobs long enough to be able to carry out the promotions year after year. It is significant that the only marketing department the author has worked with that mastered this process to any reasonable degree was one where the average length of service was in excess of five years and the promotional programme was run consistently along similar lines every year.

Conclusion

Most promotional techniques are well tried and tested. The price-offs, the competitions, the extra amount free, and the repeat purchase coupons have all been tried. In the FMCG market most promotions do not have the target of achieving a better value-for-money deal for the consumers; the objective is to increase the product's perceived value with the distributive trade and to get attention, cutting through the noise level. The promotional programme approach might not be the most effective way of achieving that objective; at least, not if it is seen in isolation from trade relations. It is, however, difficult to imagine a FMCG product with no sales promotion programmes, but for most companies it is possible to reduce the price-related promotions without damaging the sales and profit levels.

On the other hand, a cautious and comprehensive promotional programme can be a useful tool in building sales for a new product. Similarly, a programme that is carefully developed over many promotional periods, accumulating experience, can be effective in improving customer loyalty, and in inducing new customers to try the products, thus increasing the frequency of consumption.

18

Advertising, PR and word-of-mouth

ADVERTISING

Advertising is the classical heartland of marketing. A number of companies have, through advertising, managed to create such strongly perceived values that their products are chosen time and time again. All of the top 20 UK grocery brands have substantial media budgets, ranging in 1990 from £1.8 million to £17.8 million, with an average of £6.9 million (all figures MEAL).

Through advertising the FMCG companies can tell the customers about their products. Advertising has made it possible to create an imagery, a reputation, that can improve the perceived value balance beyond that of their competitors. The personality the advertising can form for a product is a tool with great potential. To quote the father of the famous advertising man David Ogilvy, advertising makes a product 'very well spoken of'. A product can gain a tremendous amount of perceived value by acquiring a strong personality.

In order to build substantial sales of a new product for a new company or a new brand, a very large investment in advertising is necessary. Such an investment needs to be evaluated with the greatest care. Many advertising and marketing managers have agreed with Lord Leverhulme's famous complaint that half of his advertising spend was wasted, but he didn't know which half.

A careful evaluation of how the advertising budget will enhance the perceived value of a product can help to isolate which half to reject or, more positively, help to increase the possibility that both halves of the advertising budget are effective.

Advertising as a barrier to entry

As the objective for the marketing management is to create the maximum perceived value at the lowest possible cost, successful advertising becomes a very big challenge. On the one hand, the potential to achieve something is enormous, but, on the other, advertising carries very high initial costs in most markets and that makes the risks high. The making of a TV commercial will set the profit and loss account back at least £100 000. In the UK a further £500 000 represents the minimum amount to get the commercial on the air to such a degree that the customers will have a reasonable chance of seeing it over a 4-week period.

The challenge becomes even greater when a new brand is to be introduced. The high initial, fixed, cost for television advertising is of great benefit to the large existing brands as they have a larger sales volume on which to spread the expense of the media investment. A new brand has a small base and in relative terms the investment becomes enormous rather than just large. For a new brand (or product) the challenge is two-fold: not only must the newcomer create a type of personality that is stronger than that of the existing products to facilitate a brand switch, it must also fund the communication of the personality and the product benefits. In relative terms, that is a gigantic expenditure. This is so because, as advertising is a fixed cost, the greater the volume the lower the cost per unit for enhancing the value. These economies of scale make successful advertising not only a method for creating a significant improvement in the perceived value, but also a strategy on which to build strong barriers for entry.

The roles of advertising

A product's perceived value is built up by tangible and intangible value dimensions. In a very simplistic way one can say that the tangible dimensions are created in the factory and the intangible ones in the advertising agency. Of all the methods of creating the intangible values, the pack design is in a general sense the most important in that it is universal. The advertising dimension, on the other hand, has a much wider scope, as there are less physical and intellectual constraints and more possibilities.

Advertising is a complex issue and it is impossible to cover it in any detail in only one chapter. From a marketing point of view it is essential to look at the different roles of advertising, to fully review the process and to do so in order to see how the perceived value can best be enhanced.

Advertising can play many different roles (see Table 18.1):

- it can **announce**

Table 18.1 The roles of advertising

Role	Communication effect
Announce	Product
Inform	Tangible benefits
Create a personality	Intangible values

- it can **inform**

- it can **create a personality**.

While the objectives of the first two roles are quite specific, the creation of the personality is less precise. It is like putting clothes on a person. The clothes only indicate what type of individual that person is; it leaves the detailed impression to be formed in the mind of the observer.

The first role, the announcement, is the most basic. Advertising a product is a way of announcing to the world that it exists. In itself that does not add any value, but it is a necessary first step as it does not matter how great the potential value-for-money perception is if the customer is unaware of the product. The role is similar to that of the primary function of the pack design: to tell the customer about the basic facts.

In the short term, especially for a new product, the announcement factor is important. If the message is credible and the product is new with a much better perceived tangible value than the competitor's, a strong announcement campaign will have a significant impact. It is crucial to remember, as always, that although the announcement and the subsequent first purchase are important, in the longer term it is the repeat business that counts. The announcement campaign must not be dissonant with that objective.

The work to build attraction, to encourage the customers to make an initial purchase, is never finished. Very few products have a constant 100 per cent awareness. There is always the opportunity to increase the attraction of a product and to remind potential customers of its existence. There are also a number of products that represent such a small part of the shopping basket that, although technically speaking the customers are aware of the product, in reality they need to be reminded of the product's existence.

For the launch advertising of Findus Lean Cuisine in the UK, the announcement factor was made the primary objective. The company was so confident of the tangible value of the products that to achieve customer trial was considered the dominating objective. If the customers would just try the product, they would appreciate the value and come back for more. This assumption was proved correct.

The announcement campaign turned out to be so effective that within six months the Lean Cuisine sub-brand became better known than most other regular frozen food brands. Although the launch was a great success, the announcement factor had an effect even more than two years after the launch. The launch commercial was kept on air and it continued to generate trial. During the launch phase the commercial would more than double the rate of sales and even after a year and a half the commercial would boost sales to a significant degree. For the follow-up commercial the announcement factor was toned down to the benefit of communicating a more comprehensive brand personality. The result was that Lean Cuisine became the biggest frozen food launch of the year in 1985 with sales of over £10 million in the first year and five years later it generated consumer sales of £50 million.

To restrict totally the role of advertising to solely the announcement of a product or service without attempting to build in any values is to waste an opportunity, and is not something one can recommend except in very specific situations. A much more effective approach is to ensure that the announcement campaigns are sufficiently broad based to give perceived intangible values beyond the strict announcement of the product.

The second factor in the advertising process – to inform – transforms the product into more of a character. It is still a factual communication, but for a product with strong tangible values the information role can be made into a significant part of the communication mix. It is not only the potential customers of capital goods that find succinct, accurate information in an easily digestible format interesting. Relevant information is by definition always of interest, the problem is to know what is relevant to a potential customer. Someone who is in the process of contemplating a large purchase, such as a car or a house, is of course very keen to have additional information. Also the everyday customer of consumer goods is interested in the products he or she uses. Most people struggle to keep a household going, and information about a product that can help in that process is useful, as are changes to and information about the products that are being used.

There are, for instance, many campaigns which, through information about additional usage of the product, have substantially increased the sales – for example, the campaign for Campbell's soup, mentioned previously. It is quite obvious, but sometimes forgotten, that customers have an interest in the products they buy. They are interested to know how a product can be used, what it can do to help them or how it can make life more enjoyable.

Whether the communication is interesting or not is much more a question of creative execution than the product itself. Just as there exists boring advertising for exciting products, there are many examples of exciting advertising for products that could easily be regarded as boring. The entrepreneur, or the successful salesperson, never thinks of products as boring. They are regarded as exciting, fascinating things that can and should be conveyed to potential customers.

These two factors, announcing and informing, can, if well executed, add plenty of perceived value. Their basic task, however, is to perform the functional duties of the communication – that is, to tell the customers of the actual benefits of a product.

The personality-building element is different to the more functional aspects of advertising. The functional communication is a reflection of the tangible values, while the personality is created in order to add some intangible value(s) to the product. A bland product (but never a poor product) can be turned into a success by giving it a real personality. The potential for such an exercise is enormous. By giving the product a personality it is transformed. The jeans, the trainers, the drink, will do more for the customers than simply shield them against the wind, cover their feet, or quench their thirsts. The imagery enhances the products' value, and with it the users' 'value' in their own, and others', eyes. With a distinct and positive personality, a product can become a very powerful weapon in the marketing battle. There are many examples of good campaigns such as the classical ones for Coca-Cola, Levi's and Volkswagen.

The ability to create a successful advertising campaign rests with two factors: (1) choosing and communicating the most appealing tangible and intangible benefit(s) of the product and (2) giving the product a distinct personality. There are many types of values that can create a positive impression and the vision of the ultimate product is the guideline for the selection. The creation of the personality to fit the benefit(s) is a task best left to the advertising agencies. Few marketing people have the creativity and skills to accomplish this in an optimal way.

The personality has to be consistent with the benefit(s) without being just a plain reflection/statement. The creativity of the advertising agency must result in the benefit(s) being integrated into the overall personality of the brand. The objective is that the advertised product – the totality of the communication of tangible and intangible values – must be shown to have exceptional perceived value for money.

There are many examples of using values to create successful campaigns, and of companies that have found the way to unlock the customers' value perspectives.

A classical case is the Doyle Dane Bernbach launch campaign for the Volkswagen Beetle in the USA. The advertising campaign(s) gave the Beetle, through a highly creative approach, the image of a reliable, trustworthy car. The car was unusual in that it did not have the accepted attributes of a car at the time: the fancy looks, the chrome and the big engine. Instead, the advertising focused on promoting the virtues of the Beetle's reliability and lack of glamour. The campaign achieved the ultimate in that it combined

- the communication of the main tangible values, and

- the building of a specific intangible value, with

- the creation of a highly distinct and attractive personality.

The car became the symbol for people who were 'too clever' to bother with the superficial standard car and, instead, looked upon the car as a means of transportation. In a highly impactful way it communicated the VW's main feature, reliability, a real value for people who had become used to poor workmanship – and the advertising developed that value to create a very distinct personality.

The message, such as the VW's reliability, is important when building the personality, but so is the media or the method of communication. The executional flair can make the personality stand out; a fairly dull idea can become exciting and really add value to the product.

The creation of an exciting personality for a product through advertising can influence the sales in a very positive way. On the other hand, contrary to what one is led to believe when reading the trade press, advertising expenditure in itself does not generate sales, and neither does image. The image only has a function when it is related to a product. The image will help to sell the product, because it makes the customers improve their perception of the product.

The extraordinary success of Nescafé in the UK was explained earlier. That success has been based on a programme of old product development. A major part of the success story was, and still is, the advertising. While the product was enhanced and made even more superior and profitable, the advertising was also improved. Current Nescafé advertising is of a very high quality. It has excellent memorability value and receives a sympathetic viewing from the advertisement-aware British public. Each week, the magazine *Marketing* publishes the highest rated commercials in the UK, and Nescafé and Gold Blend have a consistent record of being among the top five brands with the best spontaneous recall and achieve prompted recall figures of 70 per cent or more. What makes the Nescafé advertising a good example of effective communication is that while the advertising spend of Nescafé is only 10–20 per cent higher than that of the main competitor, Kraft General Foods with Maxwell House, the effectiveness rating is considerably higher.

Evaluation

Involvement in the advertising process carries high status. Many want to participate and it is also a subject in which everyone feels they are expert. The marketing function has two tasks: the first is to brief the advertising agency, the second is to evaluate the result and decide whether the commercial or advertisement is to be approved for transmission/printing.

Briefing lies at the core of the activity; it is such an important topic that it really merits a book in itself, so the following are just a few particularly relevant comments. Apart from the traditional items, the brief should also include a perceived value analysis, stating the benefits that are to be communicated, the tangible and intangible benefits that the product possesses, the benefits that are to be featured, and why. If the value balance has been clearly defined the advertising brief will be much more useful for the agency.

The building of intangible benefits is a long-term process; for the receiver of the information, the potential customer, it is a continuous process so the brief needs to contain information on past activities.

The second task of the marketing function is to decide whether the work of the agency is to be approved or not. Advertising development is very difficult to evaluate. In reality there is only one judge, the sales result over time. The problem is that once the investment in advertising space has been made, there is no return, which means that one can only learn by experience. A poor investment in a machine can perhaps be saved through a reworking of the mechanics; an investment in advertising is irrevocable.

Advertising evaluation is rarely a straightforward event. There are pros and cons with each proposal and decisions have to be made on direction and execution. The objective is to build value in the eyes of the potential consumer, so the marketing executive must constantly ask: Does this advertisement make me more interested in parting with my money? Does it highlight aspects I did not know but I would like to know? Does it portray the product so that it is perceived as superior to competition and is it generally an interesting piece of communication? There are many more questions, but they all return to the main point: Does the advertising enhance the perceived value for money?

To arrive at the correct answer, experiences from successful advertising campaigns can be a good guide. (Success equals *sales*, not awards or even press cover.) One has nevertheless to remember that the past is not always a guide to the future. It is, however, more likely to be a good guide when deciding on rejection than on approval. If something has been unsuccessful in the past it is unlikely to be successful in the future, even if the format has changed slightly. On the other hand, if something has been successful in the past, it is possible that the circumstances are now different and it may not work a second time.

Another way to acquire experience is to be aware of successful campaigns for the product category in other countries. It is possible to draw parallels and, in that way, expand the knowledge.

There are also several research methods one can use to assist in the decision process, but they all have shortcomings. Quantitative research methods are to be preferred to the qualitative ones, but one must use plenty of common sense when evaluating the results.

Advertising opens up great possibilities for a skilled marketer. It is a fantastic opportunity for a company to build up strong perceived values for a product. The investments are almost always large, so the development and evaluation of a campaign is a very serious matter. The effectiveness of the advertising depends on how the perceived value has increased, and that evaluation will be the key to determine whether a specific campaign has or has not been worth the money.

Conclusion

Advertising is a very complex issue. It opens up great opportunities for enhancing the perceived value of a product and building a personality that can make the product much more resilient towards competitive attacks. The investment is often huge, and it is irrevocable. The sales uplift and the impressions that remain in the minds of the customers are all that is left after the advertising campaign. If the campaign has been well executed that memory will have a significant impact on the value balance.

To summarize: advertising that

- announces a product to the customers
- informs of the features
- adds perceived values
- creates a personality

will generate sales, short term and long term.

PUBLIC RELATIONS

It is often difficult to evaluate the true effects of an advertising campaign, especially in the shorter term. It might be disturbed by other activities in the marketplace or the effect of the building of values might not appear until later.

The one consolation is that activities in public relations (PR) are even more difficult to evaluate. In many instances it is impossible, such as in building a defence for future attacks. If the attacks do not materialize, the entire exercise has been in vain.

In a structural sense one can look at PR from two angles. The first is indirect, classical PR; the second is the direct project-related or event-related approach.

Classical PR

The indirect PR approach is based on the objective of achieving a general positive attitude to the company by the media. Such an activity does not generally add any specific value to a product for two reasons: (1) it is rarely effective on a product level and (2) if it is to be efficient in a defensive sense it has to be done on a corporate level, which presents very few possibilities for a product-related effect. If the campaign is very strong it might filter through via the media to the customers and create an added value in product communication. This is unlikely, but at least is theoretically possible.

The main emphasis in a classical PR approach is on preventive activities. The purpose is to create an amount of goodwill (value) with the media, which can be tapped if and when there is a moment of crisis. In that instance PR has created value for the products as the PR will have prevented the products from being tainted with whatever problem exists. The contribution is one of reducing a decline rather than improving a situation. In most situations these types of activities have to be handled on a corporate level, creating a positive understanding of what a company is doing so that it has a chance of stating its views when a crisis occurs. This is not to suggest that journalists should be misled through PR, but a strong classical PR activity might make the recipients of the information favourably inclined to listen to the company's views.

The money allocated to this type of activity has to be spent very carefully as there is really no point in having a positive relationship with journalists unless that relationship is transferred into a form that will enhance the product value with the customers, indirectly or directly.

This book does not expand on the type of classical PR that aims to get press releases printed. Although that can be good business practice and can create perceived value for the product, it is only a different method of advertising. The message appears in the editorial instead of in paid space, but the principles and the effect are the same.

Project PR

The second type of PR, which is project led, can be a productive way of creating product-related values. By sponsoring or arranging an event to which the public has access, it is possible to communicate the values and benefits to potential customers in a positive atmosphere. By being involved it is possible to enhance the personality of the product.

Such an event is also quite similar to advertising, but in its execution, and in the individual way it can be handled, it becomes something of a cross between advertising and personal selling. One of the more well known of these event-activities is the continuous sponsoring of dog shows by the pet food companies. Because of its natural connection and the significant publicity, before, during and after such events, it not only creates general attraction for the products but the endorsement of the top breeders also adds intangible values.

PR as niche advertising

A specific area where PR can be useful is products with a very limited target group, where it becomes a cost-effective alternative to advertising or personal selling as PR does not have the same high fixed costs as an advertising campaign.

It can provide an opportunity not only to convey the various benefits of a product but also to customize the message. It is, on the other hand, more of a mass market technique than pure personal selling; contacts are made more quickly than through sales calls. Also, the target group may be unreceptive to a sales call, but might be willing to participate in a PR activity.

Another area, similar in spirit, concerns products on which advertising is restricted or not allowed, such as alcoholic drinks. Many exclusive wine or tobacco products have been launched through PR, as this has been both cost effective (small target group) and in reality the only permissible route. It achieves both the advertising effect and the PR value-building effect.

Endorsement

An example that represents a combination of advertising and PR is Colgate tooth-paste.

EXAMPLE   Tooth-paste has, over the years, been a category with a high advertising spend and fairly similar product claims. A breakthrough was achieved by Colgate-Palmolive, when Colgate managed to become the first tooth-paste to be endorsed by the US Dental Association. The endorsement was based on the preventive effect of fluoride. This was a real product benefit, which, through the endorsement of the Dental Association, also became a strong perceived intangible product value.

The result of the endorsement of the tangible benefit created a much improved relative perceived value with an end result of a healthy sales uplift.

That US public relations coup was later translated to the UK, but in the shape of an on-pack advertising claim that Colgate was the favourite tooth-paste among dentists' families. This was a very strong claim that give credibility to the product and added value.

The Colgate example is a good one, not only in being excellent communication examples, but it also shows the benefit of building value rather than searching for 'needs'. It is almost certain that, even before these endorsements were made, Colgate tooth-paste had a positive image with its customers, without any mistrust. The creative approach to adding value in a very competitive market was very successful, making Colgate the biggest personal care brand in the UK with sales of over £20 million and a market share of over 25 per cent.

Conclusion

PR is difficult to evaluate. Classical PR rarely gives an effect that is noticeable on a product level. That should make the marketer very cautious when allocating resources to this type of activity. On the other hand, a clever use of events and endorsements can give the marketer good value for money in added intangible value. PR, from an evaluation point of view, is very much like advertising, but carries a higher risk of error and time wasting.

WORD-OF-MOUTH COMMUNICATION

One dimension of product communication that is extremely difficult to control but, on the other hand, is potentially very powerful, in a negative as well as a positive sense, is 'word-of-mouth'. This is not a dimension that falls strictly within the classical boundaries of advertising or PR, but it would be foolish to ignore it. In the context of adding value, it is a particularly important dimension because the fundamental basis of an effective and positive word-of-mouth 'campaign' is that the customer is truly satisfied with a product.

The power of word-of-mouth communication is easily understood when one realizes that endorsements by friends and relatives always rank among the most credible in surveys. One has also to understand that such a concept can as easily be a negative endorsement as a positive one. A satisfied customer might tell up to eight others of a positive experience; a dissatisfied customer might, on the other hand, tell up to 15 of a negative experience.

Word-of-mouth becomes even more interesting when the multiplier effect is taken into account. If one can create an interesting message that impels each respondent to tell three or four friends, and those people tell their friends, then the message will spread rapidly and credibly.

Although most FMCG companies do not have a deliberate policy of creating a positive groundswell for their products, it is possible to influence the street-reputation of a product and have it talked about. It is a question of creating a buzz and making a product famous.

Two basics factors need to exist if a product is to gain a positive reputation and be talked about. Firstly, the experience of using the product must be satisfactory beyond the normal, otherwise the 'word' will be negative. Secondly, and that is where the marketer can make a direct impact, it is necessary to give the customers, the 'preachers' of the word, something interesting to say. The marketer has to provide a talking point. The talking point can be a dimension of the product, such as a most unusual pack design or a fascinating feature, or more likely the advertising or a PR event. The chimps in the PG Tips tea commercials have probably started many conversations, as has the Nescafé Gold Blend advertising with the soap opera couple.

One interesting and fairly odd example of the financial and commercial sense of using word-of-mouth as the main marketing tool is the Hard Rock Café in London.

EXAMPLE The Hard Rock Café is one of the world's most well-known restaurants. Its fame is spread much wider than the reputed 11 million customers who have queued outside it over the years. The Hard Rock Café started its life in 1971 and 20 years later the concept can be found not only in London but also in 25 other places around the world. The Café has never advertised; despite that it has managed to generate not only a healthy traffic in the restaurant but, in addition, an amazing 50 per cent of the revenue is generated through selling merchandise. In the *Caterer & Hotelkeeper*, the main magazine for the UK catering trade, the Café was named as 'one of London's most enduring legends'.

There are two reasons why the Hard Rock Café has survived where other similar concepts, such as the Great American Disaster, have failed: (1) it has a concept that makes people talk about it and (2) it has an image of being a restaurant in which it is difficult to get a table. Both have created talking points. Any restaurant where people are prepared to queue to enter is bound to be worthy of conversation.

The concept behind the Café is that it is not only a hamburger and ribs restaurant, it is a place for rock 'n' roll fans. The restaurant is full of memorabilia and, ever since its beginnings, has stayed close to the rock scene. Parties are staged regularly for end-of-concert tours, rock stars and record companies. These parties follow a determined policy of keeping the Café known as a venue for rock stars. After all, one of the greatest talking points for the target group is to have had a hamburger at the same place as a rock star.

The Hard Rock Café is an unusual concept, and that is part of the reason why it has survived for so many years and why people, today, still queue to gain entry. The name is so well known that you can see Hard Rock Café T-shirts in all corners of the world. All that imagery has been created with no traditional advertising; it is all a function of nurturing a product as well as an image.

To translate such an approach to the FMCG industry and to use it to create value might seem far fetched, but it is not. Many products hold aspects that can be exploited to make people discuss them. The coffee and tea commercials mentioned above have been subjects for much casual conversation, as has lager advertising from Heineken and Carling Black Label. Most of these ideas did not start out as potential word-of-mouth campaigns, they were created to do an advertising job. Once the idea caught on the companies in question have been awake to the opportunity and have encouraged the creation of talking points.

Conclusion

Word-of-mouth can be a very potent weapon in the marketer's arsenal, but it needs to be dealt with in a very cautious manner. The most fundamental part is that the product has to deliver over-satisfaction to get a positive effect from the activities. If not, the word might be spread more quickly, but it will be negative publicity. The other part of the 'management' is to be extremely aware of what is going on and, in a sensitive way, feed the public the kind of information that can foster the trend of making the product talked about. The product needs to be famous, and as fashion is a very fickle part of the business world, staying in tune with the customers is more important than with any other marketing technique.

SUMMARY

There are many ways of communicating with a potential target group. Each channel, be it classical advertising, PR or word-of-mouth, has its advantages and disadvantages when it comes to building perceived value. Generally speaking, the bigger the brand the more appropriate is classical advertising; but for a smaller brand it can be more efficient to focus on small-scale activities such as nurturing a word-of-mouth campaign.

In today's FMCG competitive scene it is essential to build a strong position with not only the tangible product benefits but also the intangible ones. A strong communication programme can set one product apart from another and will significantly enhance the totality of the perceived value balance.

19

The salesperson

A skilled salesperson can make a substantial impact on a business. Through an ability to find the right customers and to choose the right product and application of the product for those customers, the salesperson can effectively build sales.

The salesperson is a unique part of the marketing mix in that he or she offers a company the opportunity of a face-to-face personal dialogue with the customers. The combination of the power of the personal contact and the opportunities to select target customers makes the salesperson a potentially very powerful part of the marketing mix.

The number of FMCG salespeople has declined rapidly during the 1980s as the retail trade is becoming more and more centralized. While, in the past, it was necessary to have 300–400 sales representatives to cover the UK grocery trade, it is today quite possible to do the same with less than 50. This trend is particularly strong in Britain as the total decision-making process within the retail trade is more concentrated in the UK than in most other countries.

The role of the salesperson is, however, no less important than before. As the grocery trade is so concentrated each sales call and each sales contact is very important. The salesperson has to develop with this changing scene and have a deeper and wider understanding of the product range as buyers become more sophisticated and are less likely to be persuaded by old-fashioned 'sales-talk'.

Nevertheless, personal contacts cannot be replaced, and a dialogue is necessary to communicate the benefits of a product as well as to understand the customer's views. The company that reduces the emphasis on the sales department is very shortsighted.

The sales process

The first step in any selling process is to find the right customer. The salesperson, just as the marketer, must have a thorough market knowledge, and know where and who the potential customers are. It makes no difference whether the territory of the salesperson is split according to geographical or categorical boundaries, the key customers and the key contacts have to be identified. The 80/20 rule often applies – that is, 20 per cent of the customers account for 80 per cent of the sales revenue.

A good salesperson also has to have a thorough understanding of the customers, so that, with the help of a good product knowledge he or she can select, or 'customize', the most appropriate aspects of the products to make the perceived values stand out. The principle applies to the retail trade as well as to industrial sales. A street trader who knows that one specific customer always buys carrots and never potatoes, will of course plan a sales talk accordingly. A computer salesperson follows the same principle. A potential customer in the retail trade has requirements that are very different from those of a manufacturer of chemical products. To the retailer it might be a question of selling a check-out scanner system, to the chemical company a production-process control application. The choice of what product to 'sell' is of great importance for a salesperson's reputation. Nothing annoys a customer so much as seeing a salesperson who presents products or services that are not applicable to that customer's business.

It is also well known that a salesperson who has the customers' confidence adds perceived value through that alone. The salesperson becomes a second 'brand': communication, i.e. the sales arguments, will carry more credibility because the sender of the messages, the salesperson, will be a known quantity. That type of credibility can only be built up over time, and only a good track record will make a customer grant a salesperson such confidence. Just as it is necessary to have a product that delivers what the advertising promises, a salesperson cannot over-promise if he or she intends to return to the customers.

The key to success is to present the product in a way that is relevant to the customer. With a thorough knowledge of the customer's business, in combination with a comprehensive understanding of the product, the salesperson can tailor the communication by suggesting, for instance, some applications that the competitors or even the customer would not have considered.

The salesperson's opportunities for personal communication can directly influence the sale of a product. The communication becomes credible, adapted to the situation, and powerful through the face-to-face contact.

The objective of the salesperson in a value-added marketing sense becomes one of maximizing the product's value mix for the customer. In order to do that the salesperson must have product knowledge as well as customer knowledge.

Sales and marketing

A traditional heading would have been sales versus marketing. That is a recipe for disaster. The marketing function cannot be successful without an intense dialogue with the salespeople. Similarly, a sales department without input from the marketers will soon find its position in the marketplace eroded, the competition will take the pole position. The salesperson's situation is in many ways similar to that of the marketer's, both require a thorough knowledge of their customers and their products. While the marketer's knowledge has to be applicable to the whole market, it is sufficient for the salesperson's knowledge to be relevant only in respect of specific customers. Another difference between the two professions is that the salesperson has access to direct personal contact with the customers while the marketer's communication is almost always mechanical and only one way. Owing to time constraints, a marketer cannot have a personal dialogue with too many customers if the marketing job is to be done properly. On the other hand, the salesperson usually has few opportunities to influence the product design, the product mix or the communication package.

These similarities, differences and interactions mean that the two functions, sales and marketing, have to cooperate. This is necessary in all business situations, with or without value-added marketing, but it is very difficult to build a strong perceived value platform without close cooperation. For the marketing function it is essential to have customer feedback, and it is wasteful to ignore the salesforce when trying to acquire some customer knowledge.

For the efficiency of the salesforce it is, on the other hand, important that the salesperson has access to as much product knowledge as possible, so that all opportunities can be fully exploited. It is not enough to have access to the product knowledge. The salespeople should also be trained to use the knowledge to their advantage, which is something the two functions can develop together.

The effectiveness of allocating resources to personal selling differs from country to country and business to business. The salesforce is usually quite an expensive 'tool', but, on the other hand, it can be a very powerful weapon in building relationships, customizing the message to the customers, and closing the sales. By making sure that the salespeople are fully in tune with the principle of *enhancing the perceived value at customer level*, the results of their work will improve.

Product knowledge, customer understanding, excellent communication and a flair for combining these elements to achieve a sale are the skills that characterize a successful salesperson. The ability to use these skills and to put them to effective use requires planning and discipline. The sales call needs to be planned, the customers researched and their product usage determined, the possible product applications investigated, and the sales call rehearsed. The type of product and the conditions of the marketplace will have to determine the level of thoroughness that is appropriate and economical.

Personal selling

There are many examples of companies that excel in personal selling and, through personal contacts, establish a strong value perception. For instance, in Sweden you can only buy an Electrolux vacuum cleaner through a door-to-door salesperson. The brand is nevertheless the brand leader. Electrolux has developed personal salesmanship into an art. The salespeople have been trained to present the value of the machine to the customers, and the totality is obviously an effective combination.

The car salesperson in the caricatures is the opposite of a professional salesperson. The person in the cartoons cons and is only interested in selling once, not twice: the importance of repeat business is not understood. A striking difference to that stereotype is the world's most successful car salesperson, Joe Girard. His story has been told in many publications because of his remarkable success, which is at least partly due to the fact that he shows his customers that he cares. That care, an important part of his salesmanship, is his way of adding value to the product. His is certainly a very successful approach as most of his competitors are known for not looking beyond the payment of the car. Joe Girard communicates with his customers, and *after* the sale he fights for their rights and makes sure that they are satisfied with their purchase. Joe Girard does that because he knows that his customers come back – and it is only a satisfied customer that comes back.

Conclusion

The role of the salesperson has changed over time. It is a very old profession; salespeople have been around for hundreds or even thousands of years. The methods of how to achieve a successful sale have, of course, also changed, although the fundamental rules of customer appreciation and product knowledge are timeless. With increased use of electronic and printed media, the salesperson has been written off several times. The flexibility of the human mind and the forcefulness of personal communication will ensure the salesperson's future, despite the advances of modern technology.

The skills that are needed for the successful creation and closing of sales, will need to be fostered and developed. This is particularly relevant as increased competition will mean that the salesperson at 'the sharp end' will be under greater pressure.

A well-regarded product is always a salesperson's best friend, but he or she has to understand how to use the strength in order to build a long-term business relationship that will survive competitive attacks.

20

Pricing

Setting the price of a product is one of the most important marketing decisions made in a company. The price level will determine the revenues the company will receive, which is of obvious importance to the profitability. If the price is too low, the revenues will be insufficient; if it is set too high, the price perception might suffer and the product will not sell. The price in itself is also a part of the communication process. It is a signal to the customers as well as to the competitors.

Pricing is often considered as being easier to handle than other business and marketing issues. At least, in theory, it is a one-dimensional decision. This is in contrast to the multi-dimensional perceived values of a product that is built from many different angles. One has to realize, however, that more often than not the actual price that is paid is influenced by several other variables, such as discounts and loyalty bonuses.

The price is, first, the most public statement about a product. With very few exceptions it is the one factor about a product that is common knowledge as it is generally available through price lists, labels or advertisements. Secondly, the price is also something that is easy to monitor as it is such a simple statement. It is easy for the customers to follow if they so wish, and for the competition to record. The public statement of the price also makes it difficult to change as everyone, in principle, is aware of it. Thirdly, in many instances pricing is a politically sensitive matter. The price of milk and bread or wine and meat is something that can upset the political powers. The situation is different from country to country and business to business, but politicians and journalists are often preoccupied with prices, presumably because of the simplicity of the issue.

The perceived price can have a crucial impact on the value balance. On the one hand, the product's value mix will generate a certain expectation among current and potential customers and, on the basis of that evaluation, the customer is prepared to pay up to a certain level. On the other hand, the price comes in as the cut-off point; it determines whether someone will buy or not. If the value perception is low and indifferent, the sensitivity to the price level is high; if the value perception is strong, the price is less of an issue. This role of the pricing variable as the creator of the cut-off point makes the setting of a price not only more difficult but also more important, as it influences the number of items sold as well as the revenue per unit.

Pricing in relation to the environment

For a correct marketing view of the marketplace, it is the *relative* price that is relevant. It is the price that is perceived by the customers in relation to the environment. The customer will judge a price against

- the past

- the competition

- the general price level.

The implications of the first dimension, the past, are that a pricing decision cannot be taken without having the history of the product at hand. If customers are used to paying 50 pence, they are unlikely to pay £1 one week later. The reverse of that argument is that if they have paid £1, they will consider 50 pence a tremendous bargain.

Almost regardless of the absolute price level, a dramatic change will cause problems. The changes in eastern Europe and the Soviet Union in 1990–91 provide many illustrations to this statement.

EXAMPLE The government of the Soviet Union proposed an increase in the price of bread, from a price level below the raw material cost to a still cheap but significantly higher level. The result was public uproar. The relative price had changed too dramatically for the society to be able to accept it.

Although the Russian example is extreme, the principle also applies to the capitalistic societies and the marketing of consumer goods. If a company, for one reason or another, has kept prices very low on items that are well known to the customers, it cannot change those prices without taking the historical background into consideration. Similarly, if the policy has been one of high prices, a heavy discount will have a dramatic effect, but it is irreversible if it continues over a longer period. It is not only the past that influences the situation today; the decisions of today will influence the pricing of tomorrow.

Secondly, the general attitude to the price of a product is heavily influenced by the competition – particularly if the product area is one where pricing has been made into a strong competitive claim and the perceived value differences are small. In that type of environment a product can be considered cheap or expensive, even if the price differential is only 5 per cent. For the FMCG marketers the issue is made more complex due to the fact that they have two groups of customers: the retail trade and the consumers. The trade will treat a minor price differential on a key item as a major issue but might be much less concerned if it has to work with price differences on slow-selling lines. The consumers might react in a different way, treating the key item as an essential purchase, and may disregard a price increase as long as it is not perceived as excessive, but stop buying a discretionary item even if the price increase is quite reasonable.

Thirdly, the price is seen against the available alternative ways of spending the money in relation not only to similar products but also to other options. For instance, the price of a holiday might be judged against the price of new furniture for the house. The price of a bottle of wine may be judged against the price of a box of chocolates. This part of the evaluation can become complicated as it might be difficult to isolate the right products for comparison. The general price index can be a useful indicator but is also full of flaws. For instance, over at least the last few years the food price index has moved at a pace that is different from the regular index; and even within the food sector different products have gone up or down quite irrespective of the total sector inflation. The pricing in relation to the overall market is not something that can be ignored. It is essential to keep track of where the company's products stand.

The historic price, the price level of competitive products, and the general price level will all have an influence on how the customer perceives a certain price. The way the price is set, how it is positioned against the factors mentioned above and what the rationale is in the case of personal contacts all add to the picture of the perceived price.

Different price levels

Part of the folklore that often surrounds pricing concerns price levels beyond which the customer will not buy. The experience of many is that these levels exist, they change with time, and they move in stages. Defining these stages, and realizing what is the best equation of volume and revenue, can make a significant impact on a company's profitability.

It is always worth remembering that the profit is a factor of Margin × Volume. The price influences the size of the margin, with great leverage if the company is a normal FMCG company. With a profit level of 5 per cent return on sales, a one percentage point price increase will increase the profitability by 20 per cent (from 5 to 6 per cent). The example is as dramatic when it is reversed. A cost increase of 1 per cent will cause a 20 per cent reduction in profits.

It is difficult to quote examples of successful pricing strategies, especially since many companies are reluctant to show the full picture, including the product profitability. A study of the retail trade will provide a general impression, and is a good place to start if you wish to accumulate experiences of how the customers' minds work. The retailers have direct experience of the setting of the selling price of each product, and that know-how is utilized in pricing strategies in the stores. A field study in a number of supermarkets on a busy shopping day will provide a wealth of qualitative information.

Modern scanning technology has made pricing studies more feasible. The German market research institute GfK has published studies that support the statement that if the perceived value is strong (strong brand loyalty) then price changes and differentials have little impact. For product categories with weaker value positions the situation is different, where a fairly insignificant price change can break brand loyalties, although the pattern is in no way consistent.

Almost every company has an amount of 'folklore' when considering how much the customer is prepared to pay for a product. Unproven arguments regarding price differentials and thresholds have eventually become 'facts'. In order to make the most profitable decisions in pricing matters, the management must have a clear view of what is folklore and what is actual experience of customer behaviour.

Price thresholds

In theory, the customers' price perceptions should move gradually. In reality, the perception moves in stages. While it might be quite possible to increase a price by 5 per cent with very little negative reaction from the customers, a 7 per cent increase might be considered to be very steep. A price increase from 10 to 15 per cent premium might be totally acceptable for the customer, but a move beyond that, to 18 per cent premium, might change the perception totally. There is no substitute for experience in this matter. A close study of what customers actually pay in different circumstances might shed some light, otherwise it is down to trial and error. The GfK studies also confirmed the statement that different products behave in different ways. It is only by following the behaviour of the customers over time, and perhaps by making a few experiments, that relevant knowledge can be acquired by the marketer.

Setting the 'right' price

The perceived relative buying price, and not the price on the label, is the measure for the customer. That is what will determine the 'expense' side of the value balance. The perceived price is based on a combination of the factual situation and the impressions the customer holds of the price of the product.

These are the two relevant factors for setting the price, in contrast to what it costs the company to produce the item. Most companies would claim that the price is set with consideration of the expected customer reaction. The reality is that, more often than not, the production cost is used as the base.

The evaluation of price versus cost is part of the controlling function and is very important for the running of a business. It is, however, an analysis that should be done separately from setting the selling price for the customers. In practice, the most common approach is that the selling price is set so that the company just achieves the pre-set required margin. Although this is a practical and, in the case of simple line extensions, a fairly reasonable way of operating, it can mean that the company is losing opportunities to make extra sales and extra profits.

Successful pricing strategies are based on setting the price at a level at which the total margin times volume is optimized. Within all market sectors there are almost always specific product groups in which the margins are higher. In FMCG these product groups are no more technically sophisticated than others, nor do they require a production process that is difficult to acquire. The reason for the higher margins is that the companies involved in the business have traditionally applied a premium price philosophy and have ensured that the generic perceived value of the products is high. The actual cost of manufacture has been disregarded.

Pricing of a (new) product

When pricing in relation to competitive products there are a few rules of thumb, if one plans to enter a market. These rules also

apply, of course, to existing products but in those cases real
experiences are certainly a better guide.

When a new item is introduced, it has a higher, an equal, or a lower
perceived value than the products already on the market.
Experience teaches us that if a new product is equal in perceived
value to an existing one, it has to be offered at a lower price – not
only lower in real terms but at a perceivable lower level, which
usually means considerably lower. Very few 'me-too' products
succeed, because although it is possible to offer something slightly
cheaper, it is most unusual to be able to make it a lot cheaper,
maintain perceived value parity, and also have a profit margin.

The most important reason for misjudging this relationship is that
the producers of the new product overestimate the perceived value
of their product and underestimate the strengths of the existing
brands. There has to be an incentive in the perceived value relation
to make the customer try something new, and repeat the purchase.

If the new product offers a perceived value that is lower than that of
the competition, one should first of all question the launch of such a
product. The value-added marketing concept is based on adding
value, not reducing it. There are, however, cases in which it has
been possible to produce a product that admittedly *does* offer less
than the current market standard. In order to be successful, such an
offer has to be marketed at a much lower price. What will happen in
reality in such a case is that the new product will establish a new
market, with new price parameters and new customers. The VCR
example given earlier is a typical example. The VCRs that were
brought onto the market by Sony *et al.* were of a lower perceived
value than those from Ampex. The Japanese succeeded
nevertheless, because their new pricing strategy gave a retail selling
price well below that of the studio machines, and a whole new
market opened up. The perceived value balance became a very
attractive proposition to the new customers.

If a new product in such a case – i.e. where the perceived value is
lower than the industry standard – does not have a price tag that is
considerably lower, the product will not succeed. The customers are
unlikely to trade down unless this offers a substantial saving, and
new customers will not be attracted unless the change is perceived
as significant. Many businesses have, at various times, tried to
launch so-called 'fighting brands' – that is, slightly inferior products
at a low price. To succeed with such a concept the price must be at
least 30 per cent lower than the market level, which is not easy to
achieve in the FMCG markets if you want the company to remain
profitable.

Table 20.1 New product pricing

Quality	Price
Lower	Much lower
Similar	Lower
Higher	Similar
Much higher	Higher

In order to have a good chance of success, the new items need to offer better value and, in addition, have a price point that is the same, or perhaps at a premium. To develop a product with real product advantages, at a cost that is no more than the alternative, selling at equal price, is a recipe for success.

When introducing a new and considerably better item, the reverse of the VCR case applies. Opportunities exist for charging a totally different price. To define the point at which that new level of product superiority has really materialized requires a very thorough knowledge of the market and the customers. To use a comparison from the cars industry: when the competition becomes Jaguars and Mercedes, rather than Vauxhalls and Fords, the pricing variable changes. It is the same experience in all businesses: if you have a product that is significantly better, the customer is only prepared to pay if that difference is a true reflection of reality. For products in the retail trade, one should also bear in mind the way the trade sets its margins. As explained earlier, a new product is always at a disadvantage and the pricing philosophy must take that into account.

The price has to reflect the relative perceived quality of a product. If the product is better, the price can be higher; but if the product is worse, the price must be lower (see Table 20.1). That is the main rule, but there are many exceptions. The setting of the price is not something that can be done in isolation, and in particular not in isolation from the customers' perceived value of the product and the environment.

The communication aspects

The perceived value determines the interest a customer will have in a product. In principle, the value acts as the builder of interest and the price perception serves as the final arbiter of a buy/not-buy decision. It may seem that the price of a product is only a piece of factual information, but in reality it represents much more. Because price is so easy to communicate, it is also easy to understand; it is a factor that is easy to consider and is something that everyone can relate to. While some people may have difficulty in understanding an advertising message, or the name of a product may not be so easy to grasp at a first reading, everyone understands pounds and pence, dollars and cents.

This communicability of the price means that it often plays a role beyond that of being the decisive factor in a buying decision. The customers will often use their price information in their evaluation of the perceived value of a product. That gives the marketer an opportunity to use it when creating the projection of the product, in building and defining the perceived value.

The makers of luxury goods have, over the years, used this to the utmost. They have through experience and customer contact realized that a luxury item has to be expensive; if it is not expensive, it is not a luxury. If it is not a luxury, people will not be as interested to own it, or to use it. This principle applies to perfumes, cars, watches and restaurants, to name but a few. Similarly with gifts; it is safer (less social risk) to buy a gift that is known to be expensive than to take a social gamble on buying a low-priced item.

Watches offer an interesting example as, with modern technology, virtually all watches show the time with the same accuracy. As time-keeping is the main function of a watch, the extra value that warrants a price differential has to be generated outside of the core value. Some of the few remaining options for the creation of extra value lie in design or brand. The manufacturers have been able to create, or retain (from the old 'mechanical' days), an image around certain brands which is reflected in a higher price level, and that level now forms an important part of the intangible value for the brand in question.

The premium price in itself makes the watch more valuable. Because the watch is considered to be valuable it can command a higher price; the higher price makes the watch more valuable; and so on. For instance, a low-priced Rolex would certainly not be such a desirable item as the current, very expensive models. On a more modest scale, the difference in price between a Tissot and a Longines (often a relation of 1:2) does not reflect a difference in performance, but only in design and brand. Such a pricing policy has to be managed with the greatest of care and the premium product has to offer as much extra intangible value as possible, such as unique and especially attractive designs. This example illustrates the argument that a premium price can be used as a way of enhancing the perceived premium quality.

The counter-argument is that a low price can devalue the image of a brand. If something is cheap it cannot be of a high quality. But if the strategy is one of low prices (like the retailers Kwik-Save in the UK and Aldi in Germany), a strong feature of selected cut-price items will be the best message. If a product has a low price, it is possible that it is perceived as having good value for money. This is the micro-economic theory. It is equally possible that it is perceived as being of an inferior quality to the more expensive competitive products. Which way the argument will go is very much an issue of how the other values of the product are presented, and perceived, and how the price variable is managed. The price is, after all, only a part of the value-for-money perception to which the customer is exposed.

The perceived value is influenced by the price. How the customer interprets it, and to what extent the company can use the price as an offensive way of establishing the perceived value, depends on the history of the product group and the brand as well as the market environment. If the market is vegetable produce, the customers know that the prices will fluctuate and are quite likely to adapt their purchasing patterns accordingly. In the case of packaged groceries, the customers have a fair view of what the prices should be and act on the basis of that information. For luxury goods the price is almost part of the value itself: the higher the price, the better the value, although this principle is not universal in its extreme even when it comes to pure luxury items.

With major purchases the evaluation is often more thorough, but as the status that might go with a purchase is more overt than with smaller items, the price tag does carry an important signal to the world.

Conclusion

A general and fairly universally applicable point is that more people have grown rich by selling expensive items than cheap ones. It is equally true that the best alternative is to ensure that the perceived value makes the price a secondary feature in the selling process.

The setting of the price of a product, as expressed on the price list, is a singular action. Although the perceived price is what will determine whether a customer will buy or not, the real price will, of course, have a significant influence. This is the base for the perceived level, and has a direct influence on the success of the company as it determines the size of the revenues.

The price-setting decision has to be made against a number of factors. It cannot be made in isolation from the history of the product or from the competitive situation in its wider sense, because these factors will influence how the customers will perceive the price information. The price must also bear a resemblance to the perceived value the product is offering.

Finally, the price is a part of the communication. It is a signal to the customers, and the marketer can use that signal to give the most appropriate impression in order to achieve the best results for the company.

21

Management implications

To ensure that a new management technique or a new marketing concept functions properly, it is essential that the management style reflects the concept and that it adapts to the new objectives and strategies. Compared to a traditional marketing department, the major difference is that the implementation of value-added marketing requires experienced and knowledgeable staff. These experienced managers/executives will have to be given the opportunity to use their full potential.

The organization of a company reflects the type and history of the business. The format is a result of the way the company has operated and grown in the past. The development phase of the business, the type of human resources available, and the way in which they can be most economically employed are other factors that influence the structure. There is no need or reason to change the formal organogram because of the introduction of value-added marketing principles. Just as you do not get a marketing-led company by hiring a marketing department, you will not get a value-added marketing department by changing the organogram.

A universal concept

The responsibility for generating maximum perceived product values at the lowest possible cost is an overall company issue. Value adding and margin maximization are not the prerogatives of the marketing department; they must be company-wide concerns.

Production efficiencies and product features involve all parts of a company, and 'everyone' should have the opportunity to contribute as well as be aware of the necessities and opportunities for adding value.

One of the main points in implementing value-added marketing is that the marketing executives must have an excellent understanding not only of the marketplace but also of the products. The people who know the products are the ones who work with them. A dialogue with this 'other side' of the company can give many suggestions for product improvements. Despite the paragraphs above, the responsibility for *achieving* added value lies exclusively with the marketing department, but the *process* involves everyone.

If the total value-added concept is to be embraced by all the employees in a company, the internal communications need to be of a very high standard. People must understand their company and its objectives. Many excellent books have been written on this subject and many techniques have been floated. There is, for instance, the Hewlett-Packard 'management by walking around', which was described in Peters and Waterman's *In Search of Excellence*. There are also many other, more traditional ways, such as conferences and inter-company newsletters. The technique does not really matter, it is the general attitude of the management that will give the results.

Pride in the workplace

It is noticeable that most companies who are successful in creating products with a favourable value perception also take great pride in what they are doing. When visiting plants and offices of such companies, the pride is almost visible. This should not come as a great surprise. If you have done something well, you should be proud of it. The carpenter who has built a beautiful wooden cabinet takes great pride in such a piece of furniture. The people who build Mercedes-Benz cars take great pride in their product. A Mercedes employee, Wolfgang Rebstock, was interviewed in a Swiss magazine. A couple of quotes from the article serves as a good illustration of pride in the workplace: 'When the star turns above the floodlit building [the Möhringen headquarters of Daimler-Benz], it looks beautiful' . . . 'Daimler's a guarantee of quality' . . . 'We're manufacturing the best cars in the world.'

It is quite easy for management to get a commitment to make a product with the highest possible perceived product values if the workforce show this type of pride. Similarly, if the products that are produced are of a high quality and are appreciated as such, then pride easily follows.

The marketing department can play a dynamic part in building commitment and encouraging pride in the workplace as the marketers should be professionals in communication. By explaining to the workforce at large, and to middle management in particular, the objectives of the marketing/product improvement programmes, the company in return will have more committed workers and will produce better products.

The organization

As already stated, the organization of the marketing department is less of an issue. How it is set up is more a reflection of the type of business than of the marketing principles that are followed.

Most FMCG companies have a brand management system. This can easily adjust to a value-added marketing concept. Each brand manager will be responsible for the value relationships of his or her products. An alternative is to adapt a more functional organization, in which each manager is responsible for a specific type of activity rather than a brand. This is particularly appropriate in a company with few products.

Management style

The much more important challenge for the marketing management is to provide a working environment that encourages value-added philosophy and ensures that the company will keep its experienced marketing executives. Experience and knowledge of the market and the company are important factors, because without that knowledge the whole process of adding value becomes much slower and more cumbersome. Without a solid background it is impossible for the executives to make the right decisions quickly, and the managers then have to spend 'too much time' supervising. The management style and remuneration schemes should reflect the objective of retaining staff.

Even though the marketing executives will realize that experience and knowledge will be more useful than ever before for a successful career, the change will not take place without some management input. A brand manager who, in the past, has changed job every 18 months, will need to be exposed to a new management style if that person is expected to remain in the same job for four years.

To achieve such change, the management need to put more emphasis on motivation and internal progression within the job function. Rather than having to move from job to job to attain a more senior position, the marketer has to be able to progress within the same product area. The difference between the more junior and the more senior will be the level of independence and guidance in decision making and project work. The benefits to the executive will not only be a more challenging job, but that person will also have the opportunity to see the full results of his or her actions. If you change your position every other year, you forgo that benefit (commonly known as real experience) as it takes time for the effects of marketing decisions to become apparent.

A related fact is that continuity is essential for the benefits of a value-added programme to materialize. It is very difficult to enhance product quality and to develop a vision unless the marketing department has a heritage, i.e. knowledge built up over many years. The main reason for so many products being mistakenly launched, and so many misconceived advertising campaigns being created, is a lack of continuity among the FMCG marketers. Brand managers change jobs very often. If someone has been in the same position for more than 18 months, this is regarded by many as a personal failure. The truth is that successful people stay in their positions for many years. For instance, the two senior managers who are responsible for the very successful Nescafé business in the UK (see Chapter 11) have both been in that area of the business for more than 15 years. It is impossible to build up a solid base of knowledge quickly; it takes a few years to learn all the facets of a product and it is only then that a marketer can really make a contribution towards building values. Searching for niches without experience is much easier, but to be able to improve an existing product takes real knowledge.

There is, however, an inherent danger in this greater emphasis on experience and knowledge. While a correct view of the business world can make a tremendous difference in a positive sense, the effect of knowledge 'from the distant past' can be negative. Although it is not very common to have people living off past glories, less staff mobility will increase the risk of 'old' knowledge being used.

Management techniques

To achieve a stable personnel situation, which is the prerequisite for continuity, management must be flexible, give *responsibility* and show *trust*. For executives to like their jobs and feel that they can use the knowledge they will acquire over time, they must feel that they are trusted. The caring society of the 1990s will reinforce rather than diminish this trend.

Compared to the current situation, allowing for a lot of generalization, the management work pattern will become one where the junior people will have to be guided to a greater extent than today, and the senior less. A much greater differentiation between staff will be necessary and management will have to be more flexible. The experienced members of the department can be given wider responsibilities while the newly employed will require more time. The junior executives will not have had the opportunity to accumulate any knowledge, and in the hectic world of marketing, decisions need to be taken as the opportunities arise – hence the need for more management time. The frequent consultations with superiors will help to build up a bank of experience and then, through progression within the job, more knowledge will be acquired, and gradually there will be more opportunities to work independently.

While the junior staff will require more time, that will be balanced by the 'extra' time the more experienced staff will give management. Brand managers with several years' experience and a thorough knowledge of the product will have to be trusted to take a number of decisions without reference to a higher level. That will serve as a motivator and give opportunities for broadening the brand management role as time progresses. The possibilities to stay in brand management, in its widest sense, and to develop with it, will provide a new lease of life to many marketers.

To foster this new 'long-serving' marketing department, the management have to apply the caring philosophy of the 1990s. The caring philosophy starts with the products: all through the process of adding value, the marketers have to *care* for their products. The products will have to be treated like children: encouraged and developed to be ever more capable of taking on more demands. Just as the marketer will have to care for the products, the managers will have to care for the executives: care about what they do, care about their projects, and care about them as individuals. If not, people will leave and the continuity disappears.

The value-added marketing concept is bringing a part of the entrepreneur into the marketing department, and replacing academic analysis with business sense based on experience. To accommodate such a way of working, management must give the marketing staff the opportunity to act like business people – that is, be allowed to take decisions and be evaluated on the basis of the outcome and not on the 'political' suitability or any skilful analysis. Managing in such a spirit is really following the classical management philosophy of giving praise when successful, and constructive criticism when failing.

This does not mean that the business can be managed without systems and structures, but it can be done with less. One should bear in mind that the downfall of some promising entrepreneurs has been that they have underestimated the need for structures and have not taken the time to put proper systems in place. Systems are important, as they make it possible for the executive to know what is going on and to make sure that the company can be run 'on its own'.

The salary structures must also follow the pattern. The renewed marketing department will be less homogeneous, as there will be people with different levels of experience doing, theoretically, similar jobs. The seniors, the skilled personnel, will have to be paid considerably more than the more junior executives.

The marketing departments are also likely to be leaner, with less layers of management. More experienced executives will need less supervision, and because it will be possible and necessary to promote individuals within the job, there will be less pressure on creating management positions to retain staff.

With less staff turnover it is also likely that the total number can be reduced as proportionally fewer members of staff will be involved in training. On average, each individual will be more skilled and will be able to do a more comprehensive job.

Implications for brand management

The ultimate responsibility for the marketing function lies with the management, but if value-added marketing is to work it is not enough that management change their attitudes, the brand managers must also change. The new approach to marketing gives brand managers a potentially greater role and they will have to be able to fill the part.

It will be as essential, as now, to have a good grasp of the traditional brand management skills, such as the ability to brief and evaluate advertising and promotional campaigns. The more fundamental change will come with the demands the concept sets on product and business knowledge. In order to be able to guide the work and evaluate proposals for product value improvements, it is necessary to have a comprehensive understanding of the product, the customer and the environment.

The product knowledge must be thorough, and if a brand manager is to deserve the title he or she must really understand not only the product make-up, but also the detail and the 'heart' of the offering.

In a competitive environment, where the company is striving to enhance the perceived value, there can be no substitute for real, first-hand knowledge.

Know the product...

The best way to get to know the products, and to get to the core of the matter, is to use the products and the services. In the case of consumer goods, the brand manager should use the product in normal daily life to gain actual experience and knowledge. Thus, if the manager is working with a food product it should be prepared and eaten; if the product is a detergent, do the laundry; if clothes, wear them; and so on.

In the case of capital goods, the same applies: the car should be driven, the hi-fi or the typewriter should be used. In the service industry, the services should be used: the hotels lived in; the fast food eaten; the train stations visited. It might be difficult to achieve all this without awareness of the staff, which is something that will decrease some of the usefulness of the exercise, but not all. Even if the staff are aware of the fact that they are being observed, a learning process will take place. If nothing else, the brand manager will get an impression of how the staff thinks it should be! The alternative approach is to watch other people using the services, something that is not so easy in the product industry.

The second step is to do the same for competitive products. This will not only broaden the general perspective, but also give invaluable information for the competitive evaluation. The experience of the company's own products and those of the competition will clarify and give an extra dimension to the work of adding values to the products. As a side effect, the brand manager will gain credibility both internally and in relations with the customers. People who hold views based on their own experiences are much more likely to be believed and respected.

Is it then really necessary to like the products? This has been debated from time to time, especially in the context of client–advertising agency relations. There is no question of what the correct answer is. If you do not have a sympathetic attitude to your product you cannot succeed in marketing it. Think of the entrepreneur; the product is always liked because a bit of his or her heart is in it. Do not expect everyone to love the product, but the attitude must be positive.

... and not only the product

The paragraphs above have referred to the product. The product is at the centre of marketing and is the most important part. For a total application of value-added marketing it is, however, necessary to have a good understanding of the distribution system, the manufacturing process, the purchasing of the important raw materials and other related activities. This wider knowledge is necessary for the simple reason that you must know the business before you can improve it. Nothing works in isolation and instant knowledge gives a tremendous advantage, allowing the correct decisions to be made quickly. To be able to apply entrepreneurial techniques, it is necessary to have the same total amount of knowledge as an entrepreneur.

A period in a salesforce has always been considered an essential part of a classical brand management training programme. Such an assignment will provide a good understanding of the distribution system and the trade. To acquaint the brand manager with the other part of the product process – i.e. manufacturing – a similar period in a factory can give a very thorough understanding of the product make-up. In this way, the brand manager will become familiar with all areas that can be used to add perceived value to the product. But if any benefits are to be derived from such a comprehensive programme, the brand manager must stay with the company, otherwise the entire exercise will be of very little use.

The comprehensive product knowledge must be coupled with a detailed customer understanding. This can be acquired in many different ways, the easiest of which is to *talk* to the customers – an art that is not totally forgotten. Successful business people often spend a lot of their time talking and listening to customers. By being in dialogue with the customers, although each is a totally unrepresentative sample of the universe, you get an understanding of the real world.

The following example, showing how a deeper understanding can change not only the communication strategy but also the product features, comes from the truck industry – a very competitive market where each unit sold represents a big investment.

EXAMPLE   One manufacturing company realized that, in the decision process, the drivers were almost as important as the owners (and, in some cases, was the same individual). As the drivers spent their full working day in the cabin of the truck, their views as to what represented a comfortable and easily managed working environment were very well founded. While the owners traditionally were more interested in the mechanical specifications of the trucks and the manufacturers had adapted their communication to this, the drivers had a different view. For them, the layout of the cabin, the comfort of the seat and the handling were more important. It was realized that the owners of the trucks put great value on the drivers' views, as they knew that a good working environment reduced risks and also made the drivers do a better job. This was particularly true when the available alternatives (i.e. the different brands of trucks) were fairly equal in the more technical aspects.

The company that first realized that the drivers had a big influence on what make of truck to buy and understood how to tap this group on their knowledge had an immediate advantage. They could add value to the product by making it more comfortable and easier to operate. They then got a further advantage in that, as they were the first to recognize this key group, they could initiate advertising campaigns specifically aimed at the drivers. The truck companies were listening to their employees when they were making their decisions, so the manufacturer did the same. The end result was a better working environment for the drivers, which gave a better trucking service, and extra sales for the truck maker.

The majority of this type of information is qualitative, it is generated from individual conversations with a 'sample' that is not scientifically balanced. On the other hand, it is very valuable as it is first hand and face-to-face. It is important and useful not only when it comes to product modifications, but also in respect of advertising and other types of mass communication. Most successful copy writers have a very good grasp of the language and the mind of the 'normal' customer. Their understanding makes it possible to use words and messages that are perceived as particularly relevant.

The qualitative data must, however, be balanced with hard facts. Most companies have all kinds of sales data; data split up in different ways according to product, customer, season, etc. This knowledge must be at hand for the brand manager who ought to know it, preferably by heart, but at least should have it easily accessible. Sales data form the 'real thing' as they represent actual transactions.

In addition to the sales data, much information is usually available from market research companies. Market share information can be helpful, but many businesses operate without it. This type of information has the drawback that it is old and is not forward looking, but it nevertheless covers the entire market and is often the only way to monitor the effects of competitive activities.

Conclusion

Brand management requires knowledge. Without going overboard with new expensive initiatives, substantial amounts of knowledge can quite easily be added to the marketer's brain and files. It will not be, and does not have to be, achieved overnight. Provided the brand manager stays on the job and with the company, the benefits will soon be apparent. Value-added marketing needs knowledgeable, skilled marketing executives who will make a career out of using their experience.

Marketing management have to adapt to new situations. They will have to be more 'management' in its true sense and less purveyors of experiences and knowledge of how the company is run. Flexibility, delegating and controlling, caring and trusting are the key words for management; knowledge and experience are the objectives for executives.

Value-added marketing will change the way both marketing management and brand managers work. It will be a change to a more business-like environment with more continuity, where experience is coupled with entrepreneurship in making the products better perceived value.

22

The effects of value-added marketing

What will be the effect of value-added marketing? Just as classical marketing was not a totally new concept when Professor Kotler wrote his first marketing textbook, value-added marketing is being practised today. For instance, the system used by many Japanese companies is, in effect, value-added marketing. By observing these examples and others it is possible to predict what the effect of value-added marketing will be.

What, then, is the criteria for success? The purpose of a business is to make money, and although a business has many other objectives, the ultimate criteria for success in the capitalistic society in which we live is the level of profitability. Short-term profitability is admittedly a very crude measurement of a company's success, and the shortcomings of it has, rightly, been challenged by many. Long-term profitability is, on the other hand, the ultimate judge as a business cannot continue unless it generates a surplus.

Corporations are founded and survive because the sum of the total is larger than the sum of the individual parts. By working together, the individuals (the 'parts' in the organization) are more effective. Logically it is essential that all of the parts pull their weight in achieving a profitable enterprise. The adaptation of value-added marketing can, and should, be the marketing department's contribution to the improvement of the bottom line.

Value-added marketing has the added attraction of also contributing to the social environment. The concept is truly positive in that it makes marketing a contributor to the increasing well-being of the society. The process of adding value, making something better, in real or in perceived terms, is a much more constructive task than the constant search for new market niches to exploit, filling the shops with new variants that are not better, but only different. In other

terms, by improving the perceived values of products and services
the total standard of living increases.

The impact

There will be four main effects of applying value-added marketing:

1 *Sales will increase* mainly because of higher repeat purchase rates.

2 *Margins will increase* because of the greater awareness of costs and
revenues.

3 The *staff will stay longer*, the turnover of personnel in the
marketing departments will decrease as experience will be
encouraged at the expense of creativity.

4 The employees will be *more motivated* as they will be involved in
the constructive building of values instead of exploiting consumer
needs.

Sales increase

Sales can increase for a number of reasons; higher penetration,
higher repeat purchase rates, higher frequency of purchase or
because a larger amount is bought each time.

The main effect of value-added marketing will be an increase in the
repeat purchase rate. Through the effect of enhancing the product's
value for money, the customer will experience over-satisfaction and
brand loyalty will increase.

Earlier in the book we elaborated on the importance of achieving
high repeat purchase rates for a product, so there is no need to
repeat the arguments other than to re-state that without repeat
purchases there will be no long-term business. This, however, does
not mean that other methods of increasing sales can be ignored. The
higher attraction value will achieve a wider penetration and the
over-satisfaction will influence not only the repeat purchase rate in
its narrower sense, but also the frequency of purchase as well as the
amount bought.

The size of the customer base is one of the basic ways of
determining sales potential. The bigger the base – the target group –
the greater the potential. In recent years, one of the difficulties in
marketing, and especially within FMCG, has been to find products
with a sufficiently wide appeal. The markets are becoming more and
more fragmented because of more discerning consumers and, above

all, because of manufacturers' and retailers' segmentation activities. The trend towards fragmentation makes it even more important for the marketer to strive for the biggest possible target group to achieve economies of scale that will allow a competitive advantage to be obtained. This is in contrast to the classical marketing niche approach, where it becomes more important, first, to find the niche, then to ensure that it is large enough to carry the business.

Although in a general sense the target group for a product type is fairly fixed in size, and is not something that one can do much about, the relative position of a single product can always be improved. As an example, the number of cups of hot drinks consumed each year is, generally speaking, 'predetermined'. On the other hand, a company such as Brooke Bond with several leading tea brands can, through their marketing programme, not only influence the number of people who will buy Brooke Bond PG-Tips tea bags, but also the number of customers who will buy any Brooke Bond tea, any other brand of tea bags, or even any other type of tea.

Strong attraction values will influence the size of the potential target group. For PG-Tips, the potential universe is all hot drinks consumers, and the bigger the share of that universe Brooke Bond can make their target (and still be relevant), the greater the opportunity for a higher total penetration, and ultimately higher sales.

The value-added marketing philosophy means that one should load the product with pre-purchase values in such a way that the maximum number of the ultimate target group will be attracted. The attraction of a product has to be maximized through the numbers of potential customers and the strength of the appeal.

The ability to create the attraction is the base on which a business is built. The initial purchase must be made; the product must be tried. Whether or not there is a long-term profitable future for a product or a company will be determined by the *repeat purchase rate*. Only travelling confidence tricksters can afford to sell a product just once! A company that is building future prosperity needs a solid level of repeat business.

The repeat purchases are the most profitable part of the sales mix. A customer that has tried the product, experienced over-satisfaction, and is coming back for more, is a very profitable customer. Little extra marketing support is required to achieve the next sale. It is difficult to measure the effect, but an illustration is provided by an American bank, the Maryland National Bank. Over a four-month period the bank increased its retention rate of customers by four percentage points. The result was an increase in profits by more than 20 per cent. The higher the level of repeat business, of course, the higher the sales will be. In addition, the profit will increase disproportionally in a positive sense.

In these two cases of generating revenues, improving the attraction and the repeat purchase rate, the perceived value building must be executed with the ultimate profit objectives in mind. In the field of communication, in particular, it is easy to become over-zealous and create imagery that neither appeals to the core customer groups nor attracts people who are likely to become repeat purchasers. We can illustrate this using the example of a market trader displaying flowers on an open-air vegetable stall. It is true that flowers look much nicer on a display than carrots and potatoes. The appeal and 'recall' of a nice flower display is usually quite good; but it only attracts purchasers of flowers, and if the main business deals with carrots and potatoes, a display of flowers is wasted. On the other hand, the unimaginative street trader who just unloads sacks of potatoes, turnips, carrots, etc., is unlikely to get much attention from any potential customers because of the low attraction values. The 'clever' trader has a good display of his main goods (the potatoes!), and matches that with some attention-grabbing displays of exotic fruits and vegetables – and perhaps the odd flower to create a pleasant environment!

The attraction that a company tries to build through its marketing activities has to be relevant, but it must not be boring. To get the crucial repeat purchases, the goods have to deliver. It is not enough for the potatoes to look nice and 'be well spoken of' in the market square. They have to deliver on taste at the dinner table, and there should be no poor-quality goods at the bottom of the bag!

The task for the marketing executive is to ensure that the business builds the attractions and that the perceived values are such that the customers come back for more. The improvement in competitive strength will lead to an increase in revenue.

Higher margins

The more solid product knowledge in combination with the search for a better value-for-money balance for the customers will trim the product costs of a company. The emphasis on value for money rather than unfulfilled customer needs will make everyone more cost conscious. In theory, a better product could also result in higher relative revenues but, to be true to a strategy of increasing market share to fight off competition, that is unlikely.

The more substantial improvement in operating profits will come from higher margins. This will be accomplished through a greater sensitivity towards revenues and costs. The constant emphasis on creating value for the customer will create similar attitudes within the marketer's own company. Following the value-added principle, the activities that are chosen must be those where the maximum benefit is created for the customer (= maximum revenue) at the minimum cost for the company. Maximizing revenues and minimizing costs is one of the better ways of running a business.

In a general sense there is always a conflict in a company between the various alternatives that are available for investment in money and labour. It is an unusual situation to have sufficient resources to do all that one would like. The value-added marketing approach gives greater impetus to the importance of making the right choices; namely, those that will give the company the greatest improvement in perceived value for its customer and, consequently, the best revenue increase.

Theoretically each activity should carry a price tag and all projects should be evaluated against each other. On the basis of such an evaluation, the most cost-effective alternatives will be chosen. Followed to the letter with detailed calculations, such a process will lead to disaster, as it will be a charter for bureaucracy and hair-splitting accountancy. The spirit of the entrepreneurs must be applied. The evaluation, which is an essential ingredient in making the company more profitable, has to be made instantly and not on the basis of elaborate accountancy processes but on the basis of thorough business knowledge. For really important, expensive projects, a detailed perceived value analysis of the revenues versus costs will, however, not be misplaced. A large investment in marketing, as well as in production, requires a thorough analysis of this type. The use of the perceived value effect as a base for the positive side of the accounts will give the sales forecast greater credibility. Such a process might even make the company look at the major issues – those that will really generate extra revenue – rather than tinker with smaller, less significant projects.

By focusing the marketing activities of the company on making the products better value for the customers, the marketing people will also start looking at their own working patterns from a new angle. As the objective with value-added marketing is to improve the perceived value, the marketers will constantly have to evaluate and re-evaluate perceived product values. This means that the marketing staff's ability to understand and appreciate the importance of costs and values will increase. For instance, the marketing executive who intends to implement an advertising campaign or a sales promotion activity, will have to be sure that the campaign will improve the perceived value to such an extent that it will generate enough revenue to pay for the added costs. Not only that, but the executive also has to be convinced that there is not a better way to spend those resources. The principle is the same whether it is a £5 million TV campaign or a question of giving Tesco an extra 10p per case for a special promotion. Will the money spent on the ad improve the perceived value and thus pay for the air time, and/or will the extra 10p really improve the situation with Tesco?

The constant evaluation of the activities of the company and the ongoing discussion of perceived values against the cost for the implementation will bring about a much greater profit consciousness of marketing expenditures. This will have a significant impact as advertising and promotional expenditures often represents 10 per cent or more of the sales value.

Lower staff turnover

At least in the UK, marketing departments suffer from high staff turnover because creativity, rather than experience, is encouraged. With value-added marketing experience will become more important, and it will be obvious in due course that to be successful, in the true sense of the word, one has to stay in a job for more than 12 months.

While higher revenues and lower costs are the direct results of the adaptation of the value-added marketing concept, the reduction in staff turnover is a significant indirect benefit of the concept. It is an undisputed fact that staff turnover in the marketing profession is very high, and that is especially true of the more junior staff. The reason is that the current classical marketing environment favours the skills acquired by moving from job to job, i.e. the ability to find new niches in the market. The value-added marketing concept puts the emphasis on knowledge and experience, because to be able to guide the company quickly towards the right areas for building value, you have to *know*. You have to know the customers, the market, the distributors, the company and the possibilities. Such knowledge only comes with time.

In order to be able to act quickly, which is essential to reach a favoured position with the customers, the knowledge has to be instantly available, and the best place for that is in the heads of the marketing executives. The knowledge must not only be instantly accessible, it must also be up to date – a true reflection of the current trends. Just as a comprehensive and correct view of the business world can make a tremendous difference in a positive sense, an outdated view can waste time and lose opportunities. Only executives with substantial experiences – i.e. those who have acquired knowledge of all aspects of the business – have the opportunity to make the right decisions quickly.

With value-added marketing there will be less emphasis on the ability to find new segments and positionings in the marketplace, and more emphasis on experience. It will be less opportune to move company, as once in a new company it will take longer to be able to make a full contribution.

These factors together will mean that the current merry-go-round on the marketing recruitment scene will slow down. If you want to be successful, you have to stay longer on each assignment. This also means that the management style in the marketing departments has to change, as explained in the previous chapter.

Other functions in the company will also benefit from a more stable environment in the marketing department. They will be able to spend more time doing their jobs properly and less time educating the (new) marketing staff on how the company operates.

More motivated employees

The task of improving something is much more satisfying than trying to exploit niches. The morale side of the business becomes more positive and that, for the future, will be of much greater importance.

The classical marketing emphasis on exploiting unfulfilled needs has become less and less satisfactory. The real, major 'needs' that could be fulfilled disappeared a long time ago and the marketer has been left with either trying to construct a need (almost impossible) or trying to find a (small) niche somewhere that has been forgotten. That can be quite a frustrating exercise and is unlikely to be beneficial to the society as a whole.

It is much more satisfying to build and make a product better. It is closer to fundamental human beliefs to try to improve the lifestyles of fellow *Homo sapiens*. By adding value and enhancing the benefits that a product can bring, is a small contribution to the well-being of society.

Such a general attitude in a marketing department is certain to bring a more positive attitude to marketing and to make the individuals working in marketing more motivated.

A general comment

In addition to the four factors mentioned above, value-added marketing will also affect the business in a more general sense. In the most successful business book of the past decade, *In Search of Excellence*, Tom Peters and Robert Waterman concluded that the most successful companies were 'above all, brilliant on the basics. . . . They insisted on top quality . . . They allowed some chaos in return for quick action and regular experimentation.' Contrary to classical marketing, value-added marketing fits perfectly into the scenario of Peters and Waterman.

In the classical marketing approach, the emphasis is placed on planning and thorough analysis, not on being quick and 'chaotic'. If you follow the *new* approach to marketing, you will also, indirectly, follow the advice of Peters and Waterman. The core message of *In Search of Excellence* is that to succeed, it is necessary to do things 'better' – and value-added marketing is all about improving product quality in its widest sense. The effect of this dimension is difficult to isolate, but, if Peters and Waterman are to be believed, the end result is, without doubt, a more successful company.

Conclusion

Value-added marketing will make the companies that follow the principle of maximizing the perceived value for money more profitable. The effect will be a result of a combination of higher sales and margins, lower staff turnover and more motivated employees. The focus on essentials and the disregard of non-effective activities will make an impact on the bottom line of the profit and loss statement.

The internal operations will improve but, most importantly, the enhanced customer perception of the company's products will strengthen the competitive standing.

23

Final words

The new value-added marketing concept offers the classically trained marketing executive or manager the opportunity to fight and win against the successful entrepreneurs and the aggressive new international competitors. By using the value-added marketing approach of always striving towards improving the perceived value of the company's products, the productivity of the marketing department will improve, directly and indirectly – the former through better decisions, the latter through the stability it brings to the marketing staff and a generally better business climate within the entire company.

Figure 23.1 summarizes the value-added marketing process. The starting point, the vision of the ultimate product, determines which of the value dimensions are to be enhanced and how. The value maximization of the marketing department, in combination with production efficiencies, will result, for the customer, in a better perceived value-for-money balance. This improvement has two main effects, firstly, a stronger attraction value will generate more initial purchases and thus a higher penetration. Secondly, the over-satisfaction will result in higher repeat purchase rates (in the wider sense of the word). Both these effects, but in particular the latter, will make the company more profitable, due to an increase in sales or higher prices. To ensure future prosperity, the new additional funds can be invested in making the product values even stronger, but it may also be worth while to invest in making the production more efficient.

The value-added marketing process has to be managed on a continuous basis. If the value enhancement work is stopped, the competitors will catch up.

Each business is different, so all recommendations have to be judged in that light. What is universal is that the classical marketing approach is insufficient if you want to improve your company's profitability. The value-added marketing principle will allow you to

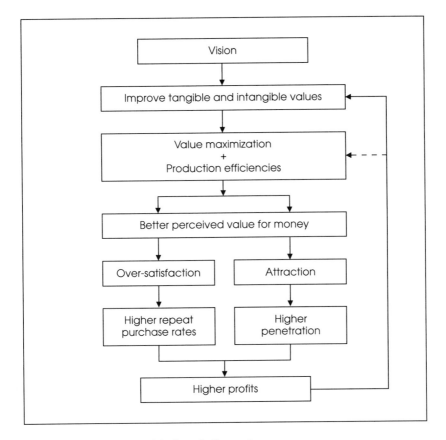

Figure 23.1 The value-added marketing system

build a marketing department that will not only earn its keep but, more importantly, will in a positive sense build a more profitable company.

Many large and small FMCG companies waste a lot of resources every year because the foundation on which they base their marketing strategies is outdated and belongs to another era. It is much more productive to focus attention on the strengths of the companies, and look at how the old products can be developed before expanding the product portfolio in new directions.

There is, in reality, no limit to how much value one can add to a product. It can always be made better. The theoretical maximum for adding tangible values is infinite. On the other hand, intangible values need to be carefully selected as mass-communication needs to be single-minded. The message can have depth and be multi-faceted, but it must be consistent, communicable and, of course, highly relevant.

The implementation of the new concept is something that will take a committed management and an adaptable staff. Although the principle in itself is uncomplicated, a continuous focus on the perceived value requires a great effort and discipline. It is only after months or perhaps years of following the principles that the full benefit will materialize. Please note that most successful brands and companies have years of heritage behind them.

Finally, marketing is a craft and it has to develop with time. There are many tools at the disposal of the marketer. It is the skilful use of these tools that will make the marketing department the motor of the company's development. With value-added marketing the process will focus on the essentials and be much more likely to be successful.

Index